SOTHEBY'S
GREAT SALES
1987-88

SOTHEBY'S
GREAT
SALES
1987-88

BARRIE & JENKINS

LONDON

First published in Great Britain in 1988 by
Barrie & Jenkins Ltd
289 Westbourne Grove, London W11 2QA
in association with Sotheby's

Designed by Nigel Partridge
Typeset by DP Photosetting, Aylesbury, Buckinghamshire
Printed and bound in Italy by Motta, Milan

British Library Cataloguing in Publication Data

Sotheby's great sales.—1987–88–
   1. Art objects. Auctions
   I. Sotheby Parke Bernet Group
   380.1′457

   ISBN 0–7126–2165–2

CONTENTS

FOREWORD

Sotheby's, founded in 1744, is the oldest auction house in the world. During its long history there can have been few more significant periods than when, under the chairmanship of the late Peter Wilson in the mid-1960s, the company merged with the well-known American house, Parke Bernet Galleries. Since then, Sotheby's has opened offices in many other parts of the world and now holds sales regularly in places as far apart as Monaco and Hong Kong besides those in London and New York. The 1987–88 season has seen many individual records broken and sales totalling $1.4 billion.

Readers of David Battie's article 'A Day in the Life of Sotheby's London', will recognize that the achievement of such a figure requires a tremendous collective effort. The sale of the Jewels of the Duchess of Windsor was a case in point; behind the scenes, as with many less well-publicized events, Sotheby's people at all levels contributed towards its success. Hard work and dedication were in turn rewarded by a result which exceeded all expectations. In accordance with the last wishes of the Duchess herself, the very considerable proceeds have been devoted to urgent medical research.

Rare organizational skills, with which Sotheby's fortunately abounds, run parallel with the labours of experts and their assistants in mounting sales. During the year, these take place on an average of six times a week in England (London, Billingshurst and Chester), and three times a week in New York. The contents of this book will give some idea of the range of works of art and related items which are handled each year by the more than forty specialist departments on both sides of the Atlantic.

Virtually every expert department in New York was involved in the auction of the Andy Warhol Collection in April. This extraordinary group of objects – nearly 10,000 in all – was astounding not only in its scope, ranging from contemporary paintings and Art Deco furniture to the now-famous cookie jars, but also in its revelation of an aspect of Warhol's life that had previously been known only to a very few. Despite his vast holdings, Warhol was still avidly acquiring at the time of his death, and as one of his friends remarked, 'Andy was only just beginning to collect art'.

Few have Warhol's energy for the omnivorous approach. In this respect what is true of most collectors is also, of necessity, true of most experts. Enthusiasts all, each has his preferred subject, as the articles in this book testify: John Stuart's piece on the Romanov photograph albums, for instance, tells of his life-long interest in Tsarist Russia, just as Christopher de Hamel's love for medieval manuscripts is reflected in his essay on the two thirteenth-century bibles.

The longer articles concentrate upon some of the more important items or collections which have been sold during 1987–88. There have been so many that a representative selection has been hard to choose. If the year is to be remembered for a single lot it must be Vincent Van Gogh's wonderful picture of irises – a profusion of blue flowers with a single white bloom – which brought $53,900,000, the highest price for a work of art at auction.

With the approach of the two hundred and forty-fifth anniversary of Sotheby's foundation by Samuel Baker in 1744, we look forward to another successful season. It is in the nature of the auction business, however, that the majority of the lots which pass through our rooms each year will give pleasure to their new owners without exciting international comment. But those that do are bound to stimulate the same excitement as their recent predecessors, the Windsor jewels or the silver-gilt service made for Napoleon's mother, for instance. We hope that collectors and armchair collectors everywhere will enjoy the glimpse which this book gives of our varied and fascinating business.

Lord Gowrie
John L. Marion

A DAY IN THE LIFE OF SOTHEBY'S LONDON

Midnight. There are no bones to disturb in the crypt of St George's Church, Hanover Square. As the hour strikes a tall – at 6 feet 8 inches, *very* tall – figure jangling a bunch of keys stoops under the low doorway. Steve Norris, perhaps the most unnerving of the team of security guards that patrols Sotheby's 24 hours a day, 365 days a year, is checking the crypt as he does at several irregular intervals throughout the night. Now racked out with grey-painted expanded-mesh shelves and cages, it houses nothing more than stationery, computer cards, files and old office furniture.

Satisfied that all is undisturbed, Steve recrosses St George's Street and is back in the main complex. In a small room hidden in the depths of the building, his ghostly image flickers across a television monitor, one of a bank that covers the galleries and linking passages. Beneath the screens slowly turning spools record the now-empty rooms – just in case. Twelve hours ago the screens were showing a tide of visitors, buyers and sellers, owners there to watch their property being sold, and dealers and private collectors examining lots for the next day's sale. It has been an exceptionally heavy selling day with five sessions each of 200 lots in three galleries, putting pressure on the computerized sale-record system. To catch up, the computer department has been working late and now, at 2 a.m., the evening shift over, the last operator signs the Late Leavers' book and goes home. Apart from the team of guards the building is now empty, and only one other movement interrupts their patrols that night. At a quarter to three the director of the British painting department drives into Bond Street. He has been entrusted with a picture by a client in Yorkshire and is now delivering it for safe-keeping before continuing home. Despite being well-known to the guard he shows his identity card, and signs himself in and out for his five-minute stay.

By eight several staff have arrived: porters with furniture to arrange; experts with a last-minute rush of lots to examine for a catalogue which must be sent to the printers later in the day; and a handful of senior directors, meeting to plan a new business-getting drive in Europe.

At nine o'clock Ernie Whipps unlocks the gilt-lined green doors on Bond Street and early visitors begin to arrive. Some have come to buy catalogues for sales, not only in London but also in the two regional salerooms in Chester and Billingshurst in Sussex, as well as New York, Hong Kong, Monaco and elsewhere. There are 35 current catalogues ranging in price from £2 to £45 for sales taking place within the month. An annual subscription can be taken out (all Sotheby's catalogues worldwide would cost £4,165, reduced to £3,125, and the pile would be 8 feet high!) but most people choose a particular specialization, such as Stamps or English Furniture.

Behind the closed doors of the New Gallery (opened in 1962) the head porter is checking each lot on display and noting its shelf location in his catalogue. When the doors are opened in the afternoon, any lot can be accounted for immediately. In the main saleroom, on shelves behind the

A view of Sotheby's Large Gallery during a view of paintings and furniture.

rostrum, are 237 lots of Chinese porcelain and works of art arranged in lot-number order ready to be sold at ten o'clock. Potential buyers are making last-minute checks on condition and last-minute decisions on how high to bid.

Nine fifteen. On the third floor of 6–7 St George Street three experts and two secretaries are on the telephone advising on likely prices and taking bids from clients. One is cancelling his bids as he now intends to come in person; others want to reserve seats or to set up bidding by telephone during the sale. This is an increasingly common practice, giving the bidder a chance to participate from the other side of the world. Sotheby's achieved a dubious first last year when an American driving up Madison Avenue was bidding (unsuccessfully) on his car telephone. In major evening Impressionist sales there may be as many as six staff manning telephones, all bidding at the same time. While this certainly heightens the tension and excitement, it slows down bidding and is viewed as a mixed blessing by the auctioneer. In a major sale he may sell sixty lots or less in an hour but the average is about a hundred; books are faster still and sell at a hundred and twenty to a hundred and fifty lots an hour (on one occasion two hundred and fifty).

Nine thirty. Colin Mackay, the head of the Chinese department, is now in the Commissions Room checking the bids and reserves entered in the Private Catalogue. These bids and reserves are strictly confidential and are written in the catalogue in code. Fifteen minutes later the auctioneer goes through the catalogue himself. One of the major pieces is a Yuan dish, painted in underglaze blue with a mythical beast and leaves, dating from the fourteenth century. It was previously unrecorded and the German owner, who had sent in a Polaroid photograph, was not a little surprised to discover how much it was worth. Unusually, no estimate has been printed in the catalogue – just the enigmatic 'Refer Department'. On major lots where it is difficult to assess the likely selling price, potential buyers contact the department for an up-to-date assessment. The day before the sale about £200,000 was expected.

In the gallery all eighty seats are taken and nearly a hundred people are standing. The sales clerk is seated beside the rostrum and experts from the department are grouped behind. The overhead currency converter which translates each bid into dollars, francs, yen and so on is manned, the vacuum tubes linking the gallery to the cashiers and the mainframe computer are tested. At ten o'clock the sale starts. The pattern of buying is much as it has been throughout this year; unusual pieces of top quality in good condition sell towards their top estimate or exceed it, lesser items or those with even minor damage may not do so well. A Tang horse makes £28,600 and another with

A view of the Large Gallery during a sale.

Clients discussing a ewer they have brought for free appraisal.

a rider £35,200 – both within their estimate – and two Longquan celadons both sell above the upper figures. However, these high prices and those reported in the press give a misleading impression of the sales; lots can be bought for as little as £300 and very many are sold for under £1,000.

The Yuan dish is the first lot of the blue and white porcelain, and there is a restless movement and an air of expectancy in the room. The bidding starts at £150,000 and in under a minute the hammer comes down at £473,000. Seconds later the dish has disappeared to the basement storage area to await collection by its new owner.

Asked to produce the worst possible design for an auction house, the combined talents of Piranesi and Max Escher would be hard pressed to come up with the labyrinthine confusion of corridors, stairs, subterranean passages and differing floor-levels that give back-stage Sotheby's its singular attraction. The eleven galleries and other public areas take up 18,500 square feet while the whole complex covers over three acres linked by more than a mile of corridors and fifty staircases. In a hundred offices staff are cataloguing, answering letters (Sotheby's receives 1,400 items of mail a day), making telephone calls around the world (nearly 4,000 come in and 2,000 go out daily) and carrying or pushing round on trolleys the hundreds of thousands of items sold in London alone. At the six counters clients are unwrapping parcels for inspection and seeking advice from some of the 150 expert staff: advice is free and without obligation. Inevitably there are disappointments, but sometimes major discoveries are made. One woman brought in what she thought was a wooden plaque; her daughter had bought it for 25p in a jumble sale. It turned out to be ninth-century ivory from the cover of a bible and fetched £220,000.

Just off the M4 motorway, on the way to Heathrow, is Sotheby's

warehouse. Large enough to house a sizeable jet airliner, it is filled floor to ceiling in apparent but deceptive chaos with furniture and carpets. Huge lorries arrive and depart daily with enough furniture to suggest that the whole country is on the move. In the cataloguing bay a thin light wavers beneath an ormolu-mounted French desk. On his back, like a car mechanic, an expert is checking the construction for alterations.

Midday. Across Bond Street in the old BBC Aeolian Hall, which now houses the Book and Jewellery departments, the Grosvenor Gallery is full of buyers attending an English Literature and History sale. The previous month there had been a toy and doll sale with Hilary Kay on the rostrum; one of several women auctioneers at Sotheby's, she is well known, as are several other Sotheby's experts, from her appearances on the *Antiques Roadshow*.

Further up Bond Street, in yet another building occupied by Sotheby's, Alex Apsis, the director of the Continental Paintings department, is working on his plans for a six-day trip in search of business, which will take in France, Germany, Denmark, Sweden and Norway. On the floor above, the shipping department is on the telephone to Customs at Heathrow, who have held up a potential client recently arrived from New York with Japanese paintings and works of art but without proper documents. Soon David MacFarlane is on his way to Heathrow in a taxi to pronounce on whether they are antique or not. If so, duty will not need to be paid and several more lots will just make the deadline for the next sale.

Three thirty p.m. The second session of Chinese ceramics has been going for an hour. At the cashier's desk two short queues of purchasers are paying

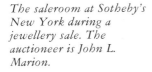

The saleroom at Sotheby's New York during a jewellery sale. The auctioneer is John L. Marion.

for the lots they have just bought. Some have already made arrangements and cross the passage to the packing room where their lots have arrived by lift from the saleroom above. Others ask for their purchases to be sent by carrier to America, Hong Kong or Japan. Dealers collect immediately for stock or to deliver to clients for whom they were buying on commission. One leaves with half a million pounds' worth of porcelain in two carrier bags.

During the day, at Heathrow, six members of staff each unaware of the others' travel plans, have been arriving for flights to Sydney, Hong Kong, New York, Frankfurt, Monte Carlo and an undisclosable destination. Some will be helping to run the 85 offices and salerooms that Sotheby's has worldwide. Others will be visiting clients to prepare insurance or probate valuations or to advise on buying or selling works of art. Last year Sotheby's Travel Ltd arranged 2,000 tickets for London-based staff and every day one was in the air crossing the Atlantic.

The flight is time gained to read a proof, write an article or juggle with columns of figures. Those flying to Europe check into hotels or into lonely flats attached to Sotheby's offices. Night comes; those on long trips sleep. Back in England the guards check each room, lock it and set the alarms; midnight returns once more to Bond Street.

THE JEWELS OF THE DUCHESS OF WINDSOR

No auction has ever attracted the world's attention like the sale of the Jewels of the Duchess of Windsor. Within days of the announcement the press were hailing the event with superlatives and, with hindsight, they were proved right. By the end of the sale, some £30 million had been raised to benefit the Pasteur Institute in Paris, far exceeding anyone's expectations.

In London, amid a welter of publicity, the BBC devoted a half-hour documentary to the collection and the preparations for the auction. In New York, where the collection went on special view, Sotheby's galleries on 72nd Street were besieged by crowds, many having to queue for hours for a glimpse of the jewels. In the days leading up to the sale itself, buyers converged on Geneva from all over the world, filling every available hotel room. The

Above. *The Duchess appears almost as a work of art in this photograph by Cecil Beaton.*

Left. *An invisibly set ruby and diamond clip by Van Cleef & Arpels, Paris, 1936; the ruby sapphire, emerald, citrine and diamond clip in the form of a flamingo, by Cartier, Paris, 1940; and a pair of invisibly set ruby and diamond earclips designed as ivy leaves by Van Cleef & Arpels, New York, sold 2 April 1987.*

PRICE
clip SF1,650,000 (£679,012: $1,100,000); flamingo SF1,210,000 (£497,942: $806,667); earclips SF220,000 (£90,535: $146,667)

Above. *Givenchy models displayed the items.*

Opposite. *A selection of the 'great cats' created for the Duchess by Cartier.*

PRICE
*total SF6,006,000
(£2,471,605: $4,004,000)*

auction took place in a vast marquee on the banks of Lake Geneva, opposite Sotheby's new offices at the Hôtel Beau Rivage. In addition to the 1,500 people who filled the tent to capacity, two further rooms in the hotel were used, each with a video link and its own auctioneer connected to the main saleroom by telephone, thereby enabling a further 750 people to attend. A similar arrangement was laid on in New York, where an auction room was connected to Geneva so that yet another 450 potential buyers could participate, as could those using some 80 telephone lines between the two salerooms. The event was covered by over 200 members of the world's press, including 17 television and radio crews.

Nobody present at either of the two sessions will ever forget the extraordinary spectacle inside the marquee. The rows upon rows of white seats, lit dramatically from overhead, were filled to capacity. Flanked by photographers, TV crews and press, they faced a raised dais on which stood the auctioneer's rostrum, floating on a sea of yellow forsythia. From here Nicholas Rayner, the Director of Sotheby's Geneva, deftly presided. In the tense atmosphere before the first session, he read out a message from the Institut Pasteur in Paris. Underlining the charitable nature of the occasion, he explained that they intended to use the money raised by the sale to build 'a number of laboratories, which will be devoted to research into retroviruses, cancer and Aids'.

The collection itself was remarkable on many levels: not simply for the Royal and romantic associations of the objects, or the immense breadth of superb quality gemstones in settings by the great Parisian houses of Cartier and Van Cleef and Arpels, but also as a unique and important document of taste in jewellery from the 1930s to the 1960s. The Duchess of Windsor was hailed by fashion writers both in Europe and America as one of the best dressed women of her day, and she brought the same keen eye to her jewels. Here were jewels of the finest craftsmanship from the collection of a woman who could fairly claim to have shaped in part the taste of her age.

Perhaps the most sensational of all her pieces were the creations of Jeanne Toussaint for Cartier, rare creatures from her 'menagerie' of panthers, tigers and exotic birds. The 'great cats' in particular attracted enormous publicity – tigers and panthers modelled so cleverly by the jeweller that they seemed almost alive when worn. The panther bracelet alone fetched SFr.2,090,000, going to an anonymous bidder. The Duchess's famous flamingo brooch, which became in a sense emblematic of the sale, sold for an astonishing SFr.1,210,000 to great applause. Appropriately enough, the panther clip with the beast astride a great cabochon sapphire, was bought by the Cartier Museum, for SFr.1,540,000.

All the large stones fetched very high prices. The emerald engagement ring of 1936 was bought by Graff for SFr.3,190,000, a record price for any coloured stone. A pair of great yellow-diamond lapel clips sold to the same buyer. The celebrated 'McLean' diamond, which the Duchess had purchased from Harry Winston in 1950, sold to the Tsuneo Tagaki Heiwado Trading Company of Japan for SFr.4,730,000, the highest price in the sale. The magnificent Van Cleef and Arpels ruby and diamond necklace, originally a 40th birthday present for the Duchess and redesigned in 1939, reached SFr.3,905,000; the necklace has the inscription *My Wallis from her David 19.VI.36* and the price perfectly demonstrated the high premium that buyers were willing to pay on all the items that bore dedications from the Duke or were associated with the couple.

It was this phenomenon which marked the proceedings the following day,

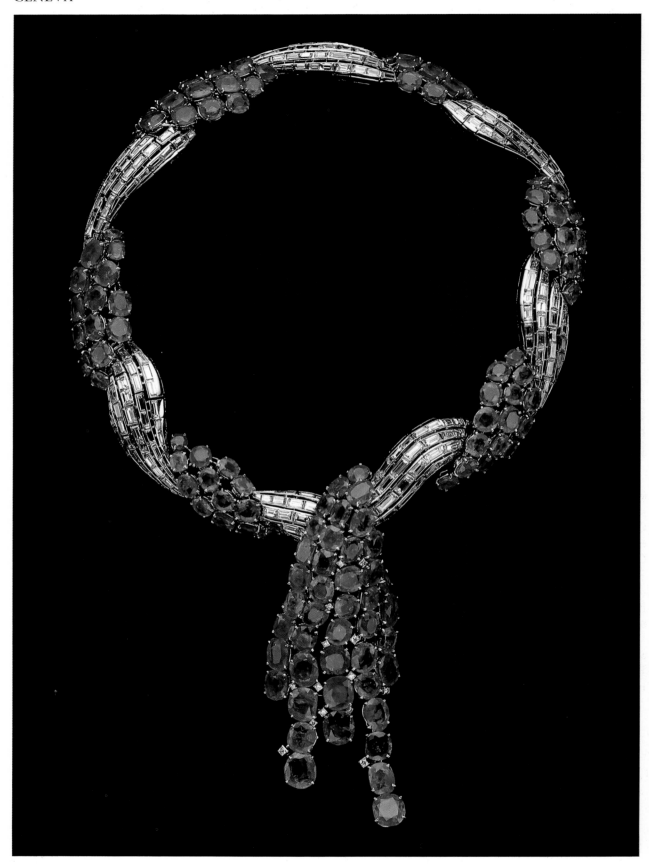

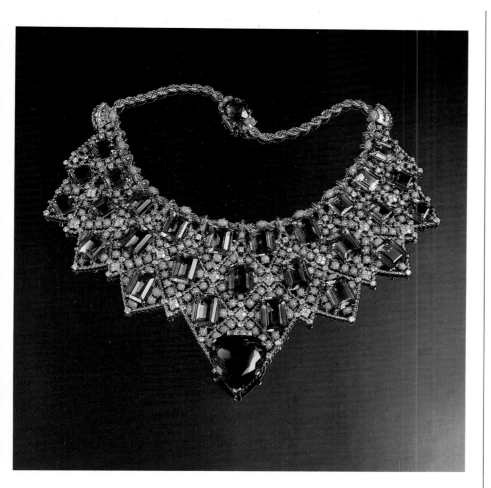

Left. *A gold, turquoise, amethyst and diamond bib necklace, by Cartier, Paris, 1947, sold 2 April 1987.*

PRICE
SF907,500 (£373,457: $605,000)

Opposite. *A ruby and diamond necklace, inscribed and dated on one clasp 'My Wallis from her David 19.VI.36', by Van Cleef & Arpels, 1939.*

PRICE
SF3,905,000 (£1,606,996: $2,603,333)

when the Duke's personal collection was offered. A Royal Naval officer's sword dated 1913, a gift to Edward as Prince of Wales from his father King George V, sold for SFr.2,200,000 to gasps from the room. A small white enamelled photograph frame which had been a gift from Queen Mary to George V on the day of their Jubilee, 6th May 1935, sold for SFr.682,000. Perhaps even more extraordinary, a small brass nameplate stamped *Edward of Wales* sold for SFr.7,700. Sporrans, seals, belt clasps and even regimental buttons all raised enormous sums of money, in the atmosphere of a charity sale, albeit on a grand scale.

The whole event totalled over SFr.75 million (£31 million: $50 million) and looking back on the two days, Maître Suzanne Blum, the executor of the Estate, was confidently able to declare: 'The mission that the Duchess asked me to fulfil has been more than accomplished.'

GEORGIA O'KEEFFE

Georgia O'Keeffe, Black Hollyhock with Blue Larkspur, *1929 or 1930, oil on canvas, 76.2 by 101.5 cm, sold 3 December 1987.*

PRICE
$1,980,000 (£1,056,564)

November 1987 marked the centenary of the birth of Georgia O'Keeffe, one of America's best-known and most enigmatic artists. To commemorate this event, the National Gallery of Art in Washington DC mounted a comprehensive retrospective of her work. At Sotheby's, a more intimate view of Georgia O'Keeffe's art was afforded by the ten paintings sold from the collection of her sister, Anita O'Keeffe Young. O'Keeffe is perhaps most familiar for her magnified flower studies, and her sister's collection included five of her most dramatic images. *Black Hollyhock with Blue Larkspur,* painted during her first summer in Taos, New Mexico, sold for $1,980,000, a record for the artist.

JAZZ

Published in 1947, Matisse's *Jazz* presents the artist's comments on a range of subjects, written in his own bold script, with brilliantly coloured stencil images reproducing his first paper cut-outs. The artist had begun experimenting with *papiers decoupés* when, in his last years, disease kept him from holding a brush. From different coloured sheets he cut out delicate plant forms or concise outlines of figures and glued them onto sheets of contrasting colours, carefully using flat surfaces without volume or chiaroscuro.

Henri Matisse, Jazz *(The Artist and The Book 200), edition no. 6/100, one of twenty unfolded stencils printed in colours on Arches wove paper, 65.5 by 42.3 cm approx., sold 13 November 1987.*

PRICE
$451,000 (£262,209)

THE TALE OF TWO MEDIEVAL BIBLES

Ancient books, unlike archaeological artefacts, are not excavated from the ground to be seen for the first time by modern man. Books have always belonged to someone. They may sit on shelves unread for centuries, but they still have a succession of owners extending back across the years. Libraries are built up and dispersed; collections are formed and re-formed. Individual volumes may be battled for in the saleroom many times in their history, and records of ownership not only add status to the books themselves but can also be significant in the history of taste. In two recent sales of Western Manuscripts at Sotheby's there were beautifully illuminated thirteenth-century manuscript bibles, each making its eighth appearance in the London saleroom.

The first was a splendid manuscript painted perhaps in Rouen around 1290. It sold on 2 December 1986 for £160,000. A year later another similar quarto-size bible made its appearance. It was painted perhaps in north-eastern France around 1220 and sold on 1 December 1987 for £85,000. Both manuscripts are quintessentially Gothic, from the greatest century of cathedrals and stained glass, and both enjoyed distinguished provenances throughout the Gothic Revival. By coincidence, they had no less than four previous owners in common, and their sale records make interesting reading. The first was sold by the Rev. Caesar de Missy at Sotheby's in 1776, when it was bought by Count MacCarthy-Reagh for £1 6s.; at his sale in Paris in 1815 it was bought by the Duke of Sussex, son of George III, who in turn sold it in 1844 for £15 10s. Next it went to the Yorkshire antiquary Edward Hailstone, who sold it at Sotheby's in 1891, for £104, to that medievalist, poet and inspiration of the Arts and Crafts movement, William Morris. The latter's name no doubt added prestige when the bible was sold at Sotheby's in 1898 to Laurence Hodson for £302; he in turn sold it at Sotheby's in 1906 for £630. Because it was returned to the saleroom too soon, the book made only £190 when it was next sold in 1909. It then passed to the craft printer C.H. St John Hornby, whose executors sold it in 1946 at a valuation of £800 to Major J.R. Abbey, in whose sale at Sotheby's in 1975 it made £15,000.

The second bible had a remarkably similar journey through recent centuries. It is not as richly illustrated and the bidding for it generally reached only about half to a third as much as that for the grander book. Recorded as belonging to Viscount Strangford, poet and diplomat, it made £6 16s. 6d. in his sale at Sotheby's in 1831. It was bought by John Wilks who sold it at a slight loss at Sotheby's in 1847 (£5 15s.), the buyer being Edward Hailstone. Like the first bible, it then passed to William Morris, who paid £60 in 1891 and sold it for £91 in 1898; then, still in parallel with the first bible, it went to Hodson, who in turn sold it for £235 in 1906. The manuscripts now passed apart for a generation: this one came to Dyson Perrins, the Worcestershire sauce manufacturer. Then it too was bought by Major Abbey (Sotheby's, 1959, £1,900); he re-sold it in 1970, again at Sotheby's, for £4,500.

The name of Sotheby's figures many times in the story of these manuscripts and it may be that the grander of these two bibles was actually the first medieval manuscript ever sold by the firm. De Missy had bought it in London, according to his ownership inscription, in 1745. In that year, on 7 January, the auction of the library of Dr Thomas Pellett took place: this is traditionally regarded as the first sale held by Samuel Baker, founder of Sotheby's. Lot 377 in this auction was indeed an illuminated manuscript bible, realizing £3 6*s*. The book can thus be seen to have risen in value 48,480 times in 240 years. At this rate, in another 240 years it will sell for £452,480,000!

A bible in Latin, with the Prologues ascribed to St Jerome and the Interpretation of Hebrew names in the version beginning 'Aaz Apprehendens', France perhaps north-east, early thirteenth century, illuminated manuscript on vellum, sold 1 December 1987.

PRICE
£85,000 ($162,350)

LE CORBUSIER – ARTIST AND ARCHITECT

M any exhibitions were held around the world in 1987 to mark the centenary of the birth of the great Modernist architect Le Corbusier, including the major show at the Hayward Gallery in London. Appropriately, therefore, Sotheby's London held a sale of thirty-five paintings, drawings, collages and sculpture by Le Corbusier in December. These works were sold by Art Forum, Vaduz, in collaboration with the Centre Le Corbusier, Zurich.

Le Corbusier always gave his paintings, murals and sculptures equal status

Le Corbusier, La Femme à l'Accordéon et le Coureur, *signed and dated 1928, oil on canvas, 130 by 91 cm, sold 2 December 1987.*

PRICE
£308,000 ($588,280)

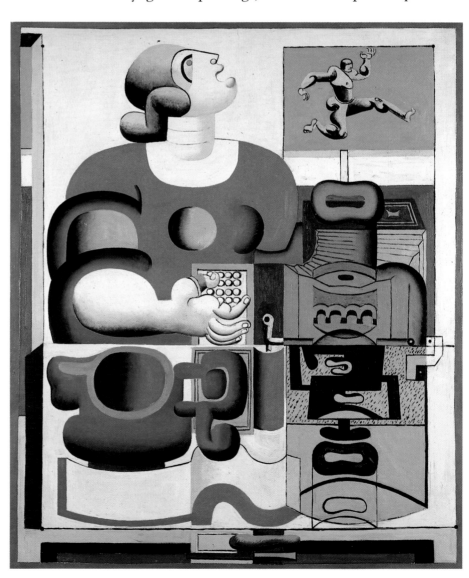

to his architecture, following the great Italian Renaissance artists. He began painting in 1918–19, for the first ten years signing his work 'Jeanneret' (Charles-Edouard Jeanneret being his real name), but from 1928 using the signature 'Le Corbusier'.

The items in the sale ranged from 'Purist' drawings of the 1920s to the sculpture *Une Biche*, executed in 1963, two years before the artist's death. It is a fluent work of interlocking curves, its shapes appearing again and again in Le Corbusier's paintings and sculptures, and even at times as motifs in his architecture. He had begun designing wood sculpture in the mid-1940s, collaborating with Joseph Savina, a Breton carver.

Le Corbusier's virtuosity extended to a variety of media, including oil, watercolour, ink, crayon and collage. He executed his paintings rapidly after a long period of gestation, writing in *Modulor 2* in 1954: 'The reward, for the one who makes a long preparation, lies in the fact that he is no longer seeking on the canvas: he expresses acquired ideas, realizes them.'

His early paintings sustained his ideas on form and plasticity with everyday still-life objects – glasses and bottles – but in 1927 he began to introduce the human figure into his paintings. The silvery *La Guitare et le Mannequin* of that year is at the watershed, the human figure parodied by the mannequin and the curves of the guitar. This painting realized the highest price in the sale. In *La Femme à L'Accordéon et le Coureur*, painted in 1928, there is a similar stylistic uniformity between the figure of the woman and the object, the runner in the background being reminiscent of Le Corbusier's Modulor man.

The Modulor was a proportioning system based partly on the human body and partly on mathematics. Le Corbusier devised a theoretical human figure – the Modulor man – and used this as a measuring tool for his architecture, believing that this would create an innate harmony between man and his environment.

From 1920 to 1970, Le Corbusier was making unique contributions to a variety of housing types, ranging from high-density urban solutions to lone villas floating above the groundscape. In April 1988, Sotheby's International Realty, in association with Hamplons Paris, sold *Les Maisons Jaoul*, located in Neuilly sur Seine, a fashionable wooded suburb adjoining Paris.

The Jaoul Houses were completed in 1956, almost twenty years after André Jaoul had first commissioned Le Corbusier to design a house on the present site; the plan had been postponed due to the outbreak of war. André Jaoul's son, Michel, commissioned an English architect, Clive Entwhistle, to prepare new designs. These were shown to Le Corbusier who, although engaged on major commissions in India, persuaded the family to allow him to resume work on the house. It was later that André Jaoul invited the architect to design a second house for himself, the first having been intended for Michel. Unfortunately, André Jaoul never lived to see the house, since he died in New York a year before the houses were completed.

The two houses, tailored to the precise requirements of the Jaoul family, demonstrate greater interest in family life than Le Corbusier had previously shown. Twisted at 90 degrees to each other, each house employs brick, concrete and timber, a combination which influenced architecture in England more than in Europe. Brick and concrete are left exposed in the houses – which are rugged features more akin to sculpture – and the vaults, supported by loadbearing brickwork, also help to give them an ageless quality.

Le Corbusier, Les Maisons Jaoul, completed 1956, sold 6 April 1988.

IMPERIAL SILVER GILT

When the Demidoff service was exhibited at the Louvre in 1819, it caused a sensation. 'It is unlikely that the art of the silversmith has ever produced anything more magnificent,' commented one contemporary critic. Lavish and beautiful services like this – the Demidoff consisted in all of 119 pieces of silver gilt – are potent symbols of the confidence and prosperity of the Napoleonic Empire.

When Napoleon was proclaimed Emperor of France in 1804, he saw himself as the heir to Augustan Rome and determined that, under him, France should inherit the political and cultural supremacy in Europe that the Romans had once enjoyed. It was natural enough that French artists and craftsmen, too, should look to Rome for inspiration, and the Empire style which emerged was a sleek but solid classicism that conveyed a sense of resplendent authority. The magnificent silver-gilt services commissioned by the Emperor and his court from silversmiths such as Martin-Guillaume Biennais and Jean-Baptiste-Claude Odiot epitomized this style, and reflect the grandiose aspirations of the French at this time.

The pre-eminent silversmith of his day, Odiot was famous throughout Europe; he made table services for Tsar Alexander and King Maximilian of Bavaria, an elaborate toilette for Napoleon's second wife the Empress Marie-Louise, and an astonishing silver cradle for Napoleon's son, the King of Rome. He was renowned for architectural designs incorporating beautifully modelled figures, as we see in the magnificent soup tureen and cover shown opposite: the gracefully proportioned tureen is supported by two winged victories clad in flowing classical drapery. Count Nikolai Demidoff, who commissioned the service in 1817, was a Russian nobleman of vast resources who had settled in Paris two years earlier. His house had become a centre for artists and literary figures and he was recognized as a generous philanthropist and patron of the arts: among his other commissions, for example, was the spectacular Demidoff vase, made of malachite from the Demidoff estates in Russia and mounted on a gilt-bronze stand designed by Thomire. The vase is now in the Metropolitan Museum of Art in New York.

Among the most important commissions for the Imperial family itself was the 'Madame Mère' service, made by Odiot for Napoleon's mother. Delivered in 1806, the year after Napoleon had given her the title 'Son Altesse Imperiale, Madame, Mère de l'Empereur', the service bears her arms, the imperial crest with an 'M' replacing the 'N'. The pieces include a splendid pair of soup tureens, covers and stands, a set of three covered dishes on stands and a pair of *verrières*. They all incorporate graceful nymphs, bacchic figures and classical detailing of garlands, wreaths and cornucopias, as well as the eagles and swans of the Empire.

The design of this service was completely in keeping with Maria Letizia Ramolino Bonaparte's view of herself as second only to the Emperor. She never tired of insisting upon what she felt to be her due, even at the risk of

A portrait of Madame Mère by François Gérard.

One of a pair of French imperial silver-gilt soup tureens, with cover and stand, from the Madame Mère Service, Paris, 1806, length over handles 49.5 cm, height 37.5 cm, sold 28 October 1987.

PRICE
$907,500 (£556,748)

incurring the wrath of her son. 'I ought to live in the Empire with the dignity that is suitable to my rank' she lectured him in one of her many importuning letters. First installed at the Grand Trianon at Versailles, she subsequently acquired the Hôtel de Brienne, furnished with priceless antiques, as her Paris home, and the Château du Pont, with its 500-acre estate, as her country retreat. But no pension, no annuity, no gift, no matter how grand, satisfied her for long. 'I require a fixed and settled income proportioned to what a dignified manner of living exacts' she told her son repeatedly. 'Your noble feelings, moreover, will indicate to you the extent of the magnificence with which you ought to surround the mother of the most powerful monarch in the world.' Thus, in 1803, Napoleon granted her an annuity of 120,000 francs, twice that settled upon his extravagant sisters, Elisa, Pauline and Caroline. Quickly deemed insufficient by his mother, it was raised the following May to 180,000, then to 300,000. A year later Madame Mère won another increase, this time to 480,000, and finally in 1808 Napoleon granted her an annual pension of one million francs.

Despite this imperial grandeur and a court consisting of two ladies-of-honour, five ladies-in-waiting, a reader, two chamberlains, two equerries, a steward and a secretary, Madame Mère lived largely in retirement, exercising the strictest domestic economy. Her parsimony became a frequent source of gossip at court. Appointed by Napoleon 'Protectress of the Sisters of Charity', she refused most applications for assistance, claiming that her allowance barely sufficed despite the most rigid self-denial. Annoyed by her frugality, Napoleon chided her, 'You do not know how to enjoy life, Signora Letizia. I have given you an income of a million francs, but you live like a bourgeoise of Saint Denis. You must not hoard your money, but spend all that I give you.' To which she replied, 'Then you must let me have two million … for I must economize, it is my nature.'

For Madame Mère's meanness had a purpose; recalling the dark days of the Revolution and anticipating the fall of the Empire, she secreted a large proportion of her allowance in foreign capitals. Thus, during the years of Napoleon's exile on St Helena, she was able to use the money she had saved to support her enormous family in the opulence they had come to expect, and to campaign to restore the glory of her son's name.

Clearly these pieces have lost none of their appeal since the selection of four pieces from the Demidoff and forty from the Madame Mère services sold for a total of more than $3 million in New York in October 1987; the pair of graceful tureens from the Madame Mère service realized $907,500, a record price for silver in America.

Below left. *Design for the handles of the Odiot soup tureen, Madame Mère Service.*

Below. *Bill of sale for the Madame Mère Service.*

JAPANESE PRINTS

Katsushika Hokusai, The hollow of the deep seawave off Kanagawa Coast, *one of the 41 prints from the series* The 36 Views of Mount Fuji, *mounted in an album, 1831–33, polychrome woodblock, 37.1 by 25 cm, sold 8 December 1987.*

PRICE
whole album
£605,000 ($1,149,500)

The album of which this picture is a part broke all records for Japanese prints when it was sold through Sotheby's by the British Rail Pension Fund. It was in near-complete form and therefore a tremendous rarity. The album included all thirty-six prints of the series entitled *The Front of Fuji,* and five from a supplementary series of ten prints, *Views seen from the other side of Fuji.*

In the image shown here, taken from the first series, Fuji is glimpsed through the hollowed wave, while three fishing-boats are tossed about helplessly on the water.

Over the past two years, the finest Japanese prints like this one have been fetching astonishing prices at auction. Each time the second print shown here has appeared in a sale, it has also broken records. The most recent one proved no exception – again sold from the collection of the British Rail Pension Fund, this magnificent impression set a new record for an individual Japanese print.

It was Utamaro, one of the leading artists of his day, who initiated this type

of portraiture, where the head alone fills the picture space, and his portraits of Japanese beauties were considered the best of their kind. Here, he portrays Ohisa, one of the celebrated beauties of Edo, who worked in her father's tea-shop. The poem, top left, reads 'The charm and tea both spill over without cooling off, Takashimaya – a good New Year's dream'. The fluid line and bold colour planes, so characteristic of woodblock technique, give an immediacy and vitality to the subject. The image dates from Utamaro's golden period, 1790–1800.

Edo, or present day Tokyo, was a bustling new commercial city. Its nouveau riche merchant classes bought prints as cheap substitutes for the more traditional paintings on silk patronized by the high samurai ranks.

Kitagawa Utamaro, Portrait of Ohisa, the waitress of the tea-shop Takashima-ya, c. 1790, polychrome woodblock print, with silver mica ground, 38 by 25.4 cm, sold 8 December 1987.

PRICE
£220,000 ($418,000)

IMPORTANT WRISTWATCHES

World record prices for wristwatches are almost commonplace at sales in New York and the three illustrated here represent the finest work of two of the most important makers: Patek Philippe and Gubelin. Men's watches tend to sell more easily than women's, which are subject to the vagaries of fashion, and at present wristwatches are more popular than pocket watches.

Right. *Patek Philippe & Co., 'Calatrava', Geneva, gold calendar wristwatch, no. 828665, c. 1935, 18 k, 18 jewels, diameter 33 mm, sold 5 February 1988.*

PRICE
$198,000 (£111,865)

Far right, above. *Patek Philippe & Co., Geneva, gold perpetual calendar chronograph wristwatch with tachometer and register, no. 868227, c. 1950, 18 k, 23 jewels, diameter 34 mm, sold 27 October 1987.*

PRICE
$82,500 (£50,614)

Far right, below. *Audemars Piguet for E. Gubelin, Lucerne, white gold rectangular wristwatch with calendar and moon phases, 1924, 18 k, 18 jewels, length 36.5 mm, sold 27 October 1987.*

PRICE
$115,500 (£70,859)

THE STUDIO OF RENÉ MAGRITTE

There is something particularly fascinating about viewing the contents of an artist's studio: like reading somebody's diary, one is entering a private realm. And it is all the more exciting when the studio is that of someone of the stature of the Belgian artist René Magritte, the contents of which were sold by Sotheby's on 2 July 1987. Magritte (1898–1967) is one of the best-known painters of the twentieth century, the most parodied, yet among the most enigmatic.

Magritte's curious imagery – bowler hats, bells, clouds, disembodied eyes – has been plundered for everything from cigarette advertisements to Monty Python. He spent most of his career in Belgium, travelling infrequently, yet he was keenly aware of, and closely involved in, major European art movements like Futurism and Surrealism. Magritte was a Communist sympathizer shrewd enough to note the corruptions of the party machine. Art was his real means of revolution and release. 'Surrealism demands for our waking lives a liberty comparable to that we possess in dreams', as he put it. Perhaps because of his smooth technique and the teasing clarity of his compositions, Magritte's work has captured the popular imagination more than that of fellow Surrealists Giorgio de Chirico or Max Ernst, or even Dali, whose personality can perhaps eclipse his painting.

Yet Magritte the man was no easier to pin down than his pictures, always sending out conflicting signals. Psychiatrists have had a field day among his works, with their floating female nudes and phallic carrots. In classic psychoanalytic tradition, Magritte rooted his desire to paint in childhood experience:

> I liked playing with a little girl in the old, abandoned cemetery of a small country town. We visited those underground vaults whose heavy iron doors we could lift and we reascended into the light, where an artist from the capital was painting in one of the cemetery's paths.... At that moment the art of painting seemed somehow magical, and the painter endowed with superior powers.

Yet when two Freudian psychiatrists dismissed Magritte's famous painting *The Red Model* (a pair of feet ending as a pair of boots), as a simple case of a castration complex, the painter was horrified by their glibness. In a letter found among his studio contents, he remarked to fellow Surrealist Paul Colinet: 'Just between ourselves, it is terrifying to see what one is exposed to in making an innocent sketch'.

Magritte told his friend and patron Harry Torczyner that he wanted to multiply his 'children' (pictures) like 'stars in the sky'. He did not hoard paintings, but was naturally so prolific that Sotheby's found a rich mine of images when they were brought in to sell the remaining contents of Magritte's studio after the death of his wife in 1986. René Magritte married Georgette Berger, a childhood friend, in 1922; she was his muse and confidante throughout a long and happy marriage. After the artist's death in

A photograph of René and Georgette Magritte entitled L'Ombre et son Ombre, *taken c. 1930, 39.5 by 29.8 cm, sold 2 July 1987.*

*PRICE
(with three others)
£1,100 ($1,777)*

1967, she left his props, letters, easel, paints, unused canvases, paintings and sketches in the studio untouched.

The sale was held not at Magritte's Belgian villa but in London, to take advantage of international demand for his work. At least £600,000 worth of items were acquired by the Communauté Française de Belgique for the Museum of Modern Art in Brussels. Before the sale of the studio contents, appetites had been whetted by four important Magritte paintings in a sale two days previously. Magritte's 1936 self-portrait *La Clairvoyance* sold for £418,000, double its estimate. It shows Magritte at his easel, looking at an egg but painting a bird. The juxtaposition of image and association had been a revelation to him that year:

> One night in 1936 I awoke in a room in which someone had put a cage with a sleeping bird. A wonderful aberration made me see the cage with the bird gone and replaced by an egg.... I grasped a new and astonishing poetic secret, for the shock I felt had been caused precisely by the affinity of two objects, the cage and the egg, whereas previously the shock had been caused by the encounter between two completely unrelated objects.

René Magritte, La Clairvoyance, *signed, 1936, oil on canvas, 54 by 65 cm, sold 30 June 1987.*

PRICE
£418,000 ($861,340)

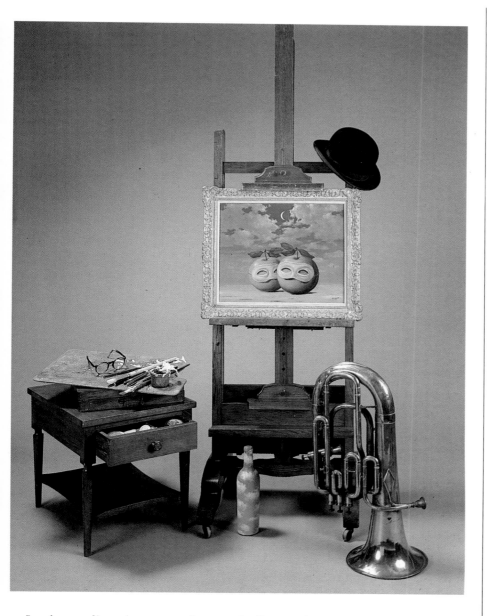

Magritte's easel and paintbox, with a euphonium and his painting Le Prêtre Marié, *sold 2 July 1987.*

PRICE
easel and paintbox £41,800 ($67,507); painting £297,000 ($478,170)

In the studio sale, an easel very similar to the one shown here, with paintboxes, paints etc., sold for an astonishing £41,800 (estimate £3,000–4,000). Perhaps it was the close association with Magritte's images that sent prices soaring, the realization that the bizarre objects in his paintings – euphonium, golf balls with eyes, bilboquet (a type of toy) – were studied from life. Magritte's most famous trademark was his bowler hat, symbol of the bourgeois whom he affected to despise, and the 'normal man' whom he disingenuously played for art critics. Sold to a Belgian collector for £16,500, it became very nearly the world's most expensive hat.

The paintings from the studio spanned Magritte's career, from the Cubist-influenced *La Femme Ayant une Rose à la Place du Coeur* of 1924 to the painting on his easel at his death, a house glowing in a dark landscape, which went to a Belgian dealer for £99,000, three times its estimate. There were also examples of the 1947 *époque vache* ('idiotic era'), during which Magritte caused an uproar by parodying child or naïve art. The highly sophisticated *Le Prêtre Marié* from 1950 went to a Japanese collector for £297,000, an

LONDON

Three painted wine bottles by Magritte, sold 2 July 1987.

PRICE
clouds £39,600 ($63,356);
fire £5,280 ($8,500);
nude £112,200 ($179,032)

René Magritte, Les Travaux d'Alexandre, signed, dated 1967, stamped E.A. and inscribed Galerie Iolas, bronze, 60 cm high, sold 2 July 1987.

PRICE
£72,600 ($116,886)

example of the rapidly broadening Japanese interest in twentieth-century Western Art. Just why this hypnotic assemblage of masked apples under a new moon should be called *Le Prêtre Marié* remains a mystery. It is also known as *La Valse Hésitation*. Magritte was very careful with his titles, which have an absurd poetry, and were indeed sometimes suggested by poets like his friend Paul Colinet. Magritte was fond of *jeux de mots*, such as the painting of a pipe with 'la pipe' underneath, that was among the studio contents. This motif developed into the well-known child's picture book depiction of a pipe with 'ceci n'est pas une pipe' below it; in Magritte's logic it is not a pipe, but a painting of one!

Another surreal joke was provided by the tree trunk and axe beside the path in the garden of Magritte's suburban villa. On close inspection these turned out to be bronze. Art, not nature, they made £72,600. Other typically Magrittian items that attracted much attention were three wine bottles painted in oils, a habit that the artist contracted in the 1940s. The earliest, a calm-faced nude, was bought by a bidder on the telephone for £112,200. Château Giscours, famous for its claret, bought the cloud bottle for £39,600 – perhaps as a lucky mascot, considering the wine grower's dependence on the sky? The recurring motifs of sky, leaves and trees show that, for all its urbanity and artificiality, Magritte's art was rooted in natural forms: 'Nature, which bourgeois society has not completely succeeded in extinguishing, provides us with the dream state, which endows our bodies and our minds with the freedom they need so imperatively.'

If Magritte's art was 'as rigorous as logic', his writing was equally lucid. The many manuscripts among the studio contents included a moving series of letters to Georgette, written just before and after their marriage, and an important group from André Breton, enthusing over Magritte's work and discussing Surrealism. There were also rare photographs: Magritte in the army as a young man, before his marriage; Magritte and Georgette; patrons like Edward James; the Belgian Surrealists. Not surprisingly, there was keen competition for these items from art as well as manuscript dealers, a combination that made for some record prices.

The sale made £2,469,434, with not a single lot left unsold. Over a thousand items passed under the hammer, revealing Magritte's diversity without stripping away the mystery central to his art. The enigma defies and entices, yet excludes no-one, for as Magritte remarked, 'Women, children, men who never think about art history have personal preferences just as much as aesthetes do.'

Magritte's bowler hat, modelled by a cast of Napoleon's death mask painted with clouds by Magritte, sold 2 July 1987.

PRICE
hat £16,500 ($26,648); cast £35,200 ($56,672)

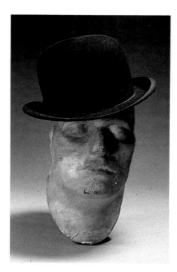

A CHINESE YUAN DISH

*A Yuan blue and white
dish, 14th century,
diameter 48.2 cm, sold
9 December 1987.*

PRICE
$1,100,000 (£683,229)

The excellent condition of this Yuan dish and its unique pattern, previously unknown, account for the sale price of $1,100,000, a world auction record for Yuan porcelain. Painted in a lovely, naturalistic manner, the fish design in underglaze blue enclosed by the moulded technique, is uncommon for the period. The Yuan dynasty (1260–1368) is probably best known for the development of underglaze-blue decoration on porcelain, commonly called 'Chinese blue and white', which predominated for several centuries. It was later popularized in the West by Chinese export porcelain: porcelain made for export to the European market from the sixteenth century onwards.

AN ISLAMIC WATER CARRIER

This aquamanile or water jug fetched a world record price for an Islamic bronze. Such objects frequently take the form of exotic animals, and this example is in the shape of a peacock, its beak serving as a spout, with another bird on its back forming the handle and providing the filler hole.

This is an extremely rare example of metalwork influenced by the art of Fatimid Egypt, produced somewhere in the Islamic Mediterranean during the eleventh or twelfth centuries. It is one of three similar pieces, which may all have come from the Norman states in southern Italy or Sicily. Although conquered by the Normans in the eleventh century, Sicily's historical and trading links with the Byzantine and Arab worlds gave a remarkably cosmopolitan flavour to the culture of the 'Kingdom in the Sun'. This was actively promoted by its rulers, who issued coinage with Arabic inscriptions, lived in the luxury of oriental potentates and borrowed mosaicists from Byzantium to portray them in a similar way to the Byzantine emperors. The style of an inscription on a related aquamanile in the Louvre is similar to that on the coinage and the fact that it is stated to have been made by a Christian would further support such an attribution. Interestingly, the present piece has a cross engraved on its breast.

A bronze aquamanile, Islamic, Mediterranean, 11th–12th century, 35.8 cm, sold 14 October 1987.

PRICE
£220,000 ($385,000)

MOZART AND LISZT

A portrait of Mozart with his father and sister, with a painting of his late mother in the background.

When the auctioneer's hammer went down on lot 457 about midday on Friday 22 May 1987, auction history was made: at nearly £2.6 million, Sotheby's had just sold the most valuable musical manuscript ever offered for sale. It was indeed a world record price for any post-medieval manuscript.

The manuscript collection of nine symphonies (nos 22–30) by Mozart, which comprised over five hundred pages, almost all in the composer's handwriting, was described in the sale catalogue as 'undoubtedly the most important music manuscript offered for sale at auction this century' and 'the longest and most important autograph manuscript of Mozart remaining in private hands ... and likely to be the only autograph manuscript of any symphony of Mozart to be offered for sale at auction'. The enthusiasm of the bidding and diversity of the general interest in the manuscript amply justified the high claims made for it.

The manuscript is in every way remarkable, except perhaps for its external appearance: it is quite small, measuring only *c.* 16.5 by 21 cm, with the outer blue-grey limp wrappers rather grubby through handling over the years. Yet once opened the volume reveals riches indeed: the general condition of the inside is excellent, the paper clean and fine, and the writing clear and firm, as if Mozart had just laid down his pen.

The survival after two hundred years, of these symphonies together in a volume of over five hundred pages, is also remarkable. They were composed at various times in 1773 and 1774 and assembled (and presumably bound) by Mozart's father Leopold, who, in an act of paternal piety, also supplied a table of contents with the themes of each of the first movements and a list of instruments. Traces of Leopold's handwriting could be found throughout the volume, adding corrections here and there. One movement was copied out by Leopold and a Salzburg scribe; everything else in the manuscript is in the hand of Wolfgang Amadeus. These are probably working drafts, though they reveal comparatively few second thoughts and revisions, thus corroborating the usual account of the famed fluency of the creator.

And what symphonies they are! No. 25 in G minor, the first of the two great symphonies in the dark tonality in which, it would seem, Mozart wrote only masterpieces; Symphony no. 28 in C major, some of whose themes seem to demand the fulfilment of Mr Bernard Levin's wish, expressed some time ago, for the composer to be canonized; and no. 29 in A major, one of the finest symphonies Mozart ever wrote and one of the landmarks of his career. Indeed, in the diversity and range of this collection, the progress of the composer from youthful genius to accomplished master is revealed.

When Stephen Roe of Sotheby's first received information about the existence of the manuscript, he doubted whether such an extraordinary volume, containing nearly a quarter of the numbered symphonies of Mozart, could possibly exist. But on opening the small suitcase in which it had been kept for many years, his reservations disappeared. From the time the manuscript was consigned for sale, he and it were almost inseparable companions.

Circumnavigating the world, they travelled to Japan and back, and the manuscript was exhibited in Osaka and Tokyo. At Osaka airport they were greeted by a television crew filming 'the arrival of the Mozart symphonies in Japan'. During the ten days that it was on display there was a constant stream of interested visitors. Mozart is extremely popular in Japan; there was particular interest in one of the symphonies in the collection, the G minor,

Wolfgang Amadeus Mozart, an autograph manuscript of the first movement of Symphony no. 29 in A major, from a volume containing the manuscript score of nine symphonies, 508 pages, the majority in the composer's hand, one movement and annotations in the hands of Leopold Mozart and a copyist, c. 1773–74, sold 22 May 1987.

PRICE
£2,585,000 ($4,575,450)

which had featured prominently in the film *Amadeus*. During the exhibition in Tokyo one man came in every day to see a new page of the manuscript. It received a similar amount of interest and enthusiasm when it was exhibited in London and New York.

A large number of musicians, conductors and musicologists visited the exhibitions, and many had interesting remarks to make about the exhibit. After spending a considerable time examining the manuscript, one distinguished conductor announced that now he knew how to conduct the symphonies. A composer's manuscript contains nuances of expression and performance information which are absent in the impersonal layout of a printed score. To listen to a work from the original manuscript is about the most exciting and revealing thing a musician can do. Somehow, few recorded performances come up to the mark of the original.

The day of the sale itself was unusually hectic, with the room packed with television crews, hot television lights, and a plethora of people wishing to catch a final glance of the manuscript, telephone hook-ups to be arranged and bidders in the room to be accommodated. When the hammer went down, the purchaser raced out of the room pursued by a posse of press.

The manuscript went to an American collection where it will, it is understood, be on display at the Pierpont Morgan Library, New York.

In the following auction of music, on 27 November 1987, another important manuscript was offered for sale. This was a discovery of an apparently new and unknown piano work by Franz Liszt (1811–1886). Without title or signature, the manuscript is of a large-scale piano work, a fantasia based on a 'Chansonette'. The central, slow section consists of a passage later used as the main material of 'La chapelle de Guillaume Tell', one of Liszt's most justly famous and magical compositions, published in the *Années de Pèlerinage/Album d'un voyageur* collections (*c.* 1839). The thirty-six pages, heavily worked by the composer, contain extensive revisions and alterations, and this is quite clearly a 'composition' score.

The output of Liszt is still, one hundred years after the composer's death, fraught with error and confusion, and no modern, up-to-date thematic catalogue of his works exists. There are well over seven hundred pieces to his name, many of them revised, transformed and republished in new versions in later years (Liszt's music was printed by over one hundred publishers in his own lifetime). A number remain unpublished, surviving in libraries with restricted access. So what with various misattributed pieces, an extensive literature on the composer (not always of the highest quality), and manuscript sources scattered around the world in places as far apart as Leningrad and South America, to establish the credentials of this new manuscript was not easy.

On the evidence of the handwriting, it would appear to date from early in his career, probably from the early 1830s, when Liszt was travelling throughout Europe as a piano virtuoso, a period from which relatively few works survive. The composition was unknown to the Franz Liszt Academy in Budapest and to scholars working on the new edition of the composer's works, as well as to many other Liszt authorities to whom the manuscript was shown.

Sotheby's came to the conclusion that it was almost certainly the lost 'Grand Solo caractéristique à propos d'une chansonette de Panseron', mentioned by Liszt in a letter of 12 December 1832. Auguste Panseron was a singer and composer who had staged concerts in which Liszt performed in the late 1820s and early 1830s. An examination of the available publications

JOHN VOOS

Dr Stephen Roe, of Sotheby's, performs from the manuscript beneath a portrait of Liszt at the Steinway showroom, London.

Lost Liszt manuscript reappears

By Fiona Maddocks

AN IMPORTANT early piano work by Liszt, hitherto unknown and unpublished, has been discovered by Sotheby's almost 160 years after being written. The manuscript, 36 pages long and notated swiftly and untidily in brown ink on two types of paper, has no title, signature or date, but Liszt scholars have no doubt as to its authorship. It was acquired from a private owner who lives abroad.

Dr Stephen Roe, a director in Sotheby's Department of Manuscripts, has indentified it as Liszt's lost *Grand Solo caractéristique à propos d'une chansonette de Panseron*, mentioned by the composer only once, in a letter dated 12 Decem-

Part of the newly-discovered score, written about 160 years ago.

ber 1832. "It's an entirely new work, and one which seems to have escaped any worklist of his music. In form and structure, it's as revolutionary and forward-looking as any of the important works he wrote in the late 1830s," Dr Roe said.

The work dates from around

1830, a period when the 19-year-old Liszt composed little, debilitated by a failed love affair, by religious fervour, and by the pressures of life as a celebrated pianist. It is a full-blooded romantic fantasy lasting around 15 minutes, bearing all Liszt's hallmarks and annotated closely

with instructions to play "furiously", "with fire", and "desperately".

Whole passages are scrubbed out, corrections added on slips of paper affixed to the orginal. The significant central section, marked *Larghetto religioso*, contains close reference to the later *La Chapelle de Guillaume Tell* from the *Anées de Pelerinage*.

Lost manuscripts by Liszt are not in themselves rare. Many of his 700 or so works, often revisions of his own compositions or plunderings of those by other composers, have disappeared since his death in 1886.

But this is the first time a work has come to light whose existence was previously unknown, and the manuscript is expected to fetch £40,000-£60,000 when it goes for auction next month.

An article on the front page of The Independent *on 30 October 1987 told the story of the reappearance of the Liszt manuscript, and showed a photograph of Sotheby's expert Stephen Roe playing the score on the piano.*

of Panseron has not yet uncovered the 'Chansonette' upon which the piano work is based, but on stylistic grounds there are many similarities.

The discovery created a great deal of interest in the press, on the radio and on television. On the day of the sale, enthusiastic bidding resulted in a sale price of £77,000 (including premium), against an estimate of £40,000–60,000.

AMERICAN PAINTINGS FROM THE FOULKE COLLECTION

Caroline Ryan Foulke

Caroline Ryan Foulke was the granddaughter of Thomas Fortune Ryan, one of the great financial figures of the Gilded Age. Born in Lovingston, Virginia, Ryan was orphaned at an early age and moved to Baltimore to seek his fortune. He soon found a job as an errand-boy for John S. Barry, a dry-goods merchant. In 1872 he moved to New York to work as a messenger on Wall Street and in only two years he had secured himself a seat on the Stock Exchange, having married Ida Barry, the daughter of his former employer. By 1906 he was worth an estimated $50 million, in those days an astounding sum, and had major interests in tobacco, insurance, banking and the New York streetcar system. King Leopold of Belgium asked him to develop the natural resources of the Congo and, as a result, his fortune increased sixfold in six years. In his home town of Lovingston, he built Oak Ridge, a 5,000-acre farm complete with a hot-house, a private railway station, and a cinema which was opened to the public on Saturdays. His wife was a devout Catholic and he erected for her benefit the magnificent Saint Jean Baptiste Church on Lexington Avenue in New York.

Despite all this, Ryan had the time to collect art, and to collect with distinction in the same meticulous fashion in which he had made his fortune. Without the aid of any expert advice, he formed a collection of great variety and breadth, not only in the areas then fashionable, such as Renaissance furnishings and decorative arts, but also in more unusual fields such as Etruscan bronzes. His collection of Limoges enamels was especially fine.

Caroline was very much of her grandfather's energetic mettle. Born on 8 April 1910, she was brought up in New York amidst all of the Ryan splendour, and spent her summers at Oak Ridge. In New York she became increasingly interested in art history and in travel and was to make frequent trips to Europe, particularly Baden-Baden and Paris, for the rest of her life. Yachting and yachting parties attracted her, and later in life she purchased Harold Vanderbilt's yacht *Versatile*.

During the Second World War, Caroline volunteered to become a nurse in the Red Cross. Suspecting that she would be sent to the South Pacific, she packed supplies so that she could fish to sustain herself on a tropical island if necessary. She was sent, however, to London. Once on the *Queen Mary* she became the centre of attention, not only for her stunning looks but for her elegant bearing. In London, with typical *élan*, she wore a mink coat over her nurse's uniform and after hours acted as a hostess for the officers' club or held parties for enlisted men at her suite at the Ritz. She seems to have become interested in American paintings at the end of the War and started collecting in about 1947. In a relatively short time, with guidance from the Macbeth Gallery and Jay Russek of Wildenstein, she had amassed an impressive collection.

Of the seven works offered for sale last year, only one artist was represented by more than one painting – James McNeill Whistler. A charming watercolour entitled *Beach at Dieppe*, dating from *c.* 1884, was a fine example of the artist's use of Japanese-inspired composition with spirited calligraphic brushstrokes to produce a wonderfully shimmering effect. The more important painting, however, was an oil. Painted in 1871, *Variations in Violet and Green* was produced at a time of transition in Whistler's career. It depicts the embankment of the Thames at Battersea Reach, with a group of three elegant ladies in the narrow foreground, and the serene river at sunset stretching out beyond. Painted thinly in broad strokes of soft, rich colour, it begins to turn away from the earlier, Graeco-Japanese

James McNeill Whistler, Variations in Violet and Green, *1871, oil on canvas, 61 by 35.5 cm, sold 28 May 1987.*

PRICE
$2,585,000 (£1,557,229)

style of painting Whistler had employed in the 1860s and towards the more purely oriental style of the 1870s, especially presaging the famous Thames *Nocturnes* of that decade. The painting was done during the same summer that Whistler painted what is probably his best-known work, *Arrangement in Grey and Black*, popularly known as *Whistler's Mother*, now in the Louvre. When shown in the 5th Winter Exhibition of Cabinet Pictures in Oil in 1871, *Variations in Violet and Green* was highly praised for its expressive qualities and its colouration. At a distance of over a hundred years, perhaps we have a better view of its importance and beauty than did the critic who offered that modest appraisal. The first major Whistler oil to appear at auction since the 1940s, it made $2,585,000, one of the highest prices for an American painting at auction.

Painted just two years later, Winslow Homer's watercolour *In Charge of Baby* provided the perfect foil for *Variations*. A bright, jewel-like picture, it depicts children tending their baby sister rather than fashionable ladies strolling along the waterfront. Although Homer is now regarded as one of America's leading watercolourists, he did not work in the medium seriously until relatively late in life. *In Charge of Baby* was one of a series celebrating the innocence of childhood that he painted during a summer holiday in Gloucester, Massachusetts, in 1873. These were his first real essays in watercolour. Up to that point watercolours had been regarded in America as 'fit for girls and amateurs', but this prejudice had begun to change as a result of a special exhibition mounted by the American Society of Painters in Water Colors earlier that year. Altogether devoid of the dreamlike quality apparent in Whistler, Homer's naturalistic and frank style was well suited to the immediacy of watercolour. This quality was no doubt sharpened by his early training as a journalistic artist for *Harper's Weekly* and other such publications. *In Charge of Baby*, full of vibrancy and charm, brought a record price for an American watercolour – $770,000.

Another aspect of Mrs Foulke's taste was reflected in Thomas Eakins's portrait *The Art Student – Portrait of James Wright* of 1890. Unlike most portraitists of the Belle Epoque, Eakins kept his embellishments sparse, his composition simple and his forms highly sculptural. *The Art Student* is a fine example of this. Painted in the rich but sombre tones that Eakins so often favoured, its deeply meditative and psychological tone brings it close in flavour to the best portraits of the seventeenth-century Dutch School. Certainly it must have stood out from all of the Sargent, Boldini, and Helleu

Winslow Homer, In Charge of Baby, *1873, watercolour on paper, 21.6 by 34.4 cm, sold 28 May 1987.*

PRICE
$770,000 (£463,855)

imitations that were being produced at the time. The composition reflects
Eakins's use of the camera as a tool of the artist: the viewpoint, the pose of
the figure, and the matter-of-factness are all photographic. One of many
masterpieces by Eakins to have been rejected by exhibition juries only to be
'rediscovered' at a later date, this painting was sold for a record $2,420,000.

A FEUILLES DE CHOUX *TAPESTRY*

A Flemish feuilles de choux *tapestry panel, Enghien or Grammont, c. 1550, 234 by 366 cm, sold 30 May 1987.*

PRICE
$121,000 (£72,892)

By the early sixteenth century the Low Countries were the unrivalled centre of tapestry manufacture in Europe, the industry being concentrated above all in Brussels, but with workshops in many other towns. This *feuilles de choux* tapestry, which fetched $121,000, was made in Enghien or Grammont *c.* 1550. The *feuilles de choux* motif, a lush arrangement of overscaled, scrolling cabbage leaves, was introduced to these weaving centres during the mid-sixteenth century, only to disappear abruptly about fifty years later. The imagery combines traditional fifteenth-century elements – the lion and the horse amid foliage and fruit – with maize and tropical parrots, known only after the discovery of the New World.

THE REBUKE OF ADAM AND EVE

T his version of the *Rebuke of Adam and Eve* is the largest of Domenichino's three paintings of the subject. Works by this seventeenth-century Emilian artist rarely appear on the market, and this example brought a world record price.

Domenico Zampieri, called Domenichino, The Rebuke of Adam and Eve, *oil on canvas, 122 by 172 cm, sold 4 June 1987.*

PRICE
$1,540,000 (£944,785)

THE DRAEGER COLLECTION OF FIREARMS

C harles Draeger was born in Paris on 12 November 1899, into a family established as eminent art printers. They expected him to help in the business from an early age, and there can be little doubt that the firm's production of exclusive prints by Dufy, Matisse, Dali, Picasso and others developed his taste and connoisseurship.

The family history also offers an intriguing insight into the military theme that would become so significant to Charles. His great-grandfather was rescued from the Turks by Napoleon's bodyguard and became a standard-bearer in the Imperial Guard. Receiving 27 wounds in the ensuing campaigns, he was rewarded with the Legion d'Honneur. With such a military background, Charles was chagrined to find himself debarred by age from action in the First World War; although he served in Morocco soon afterwards. In his collecting, Charles Draeger found himself called to arms in a different sense. His superlative collection of antique firearms was auctioned in Monaco last December. Almost unknown to authorities in this field, it contained lot after lot of top-quality items – arms of historical importance, of royal provenance, or simply of outstanding craftsmanship.

One of the most interesting items was a sword presented by Napoleon to General Desaix. The occasion, in 1799, was the French conquest of Upper Egypt. Elaborately decorated and in the form of an Indian *talwar*, the sword is traditionally supposed to have been taken from a British soldier during the Battle of the Pyramids, but on stylistic grounds it is more probably of French

A talwar with silver-gilt and enamelled mounts, inscribed, late 18th century, 94.5 cm, from the Draeger Collection, sold 7 December 1987.

PRICE
FF355,200 (£35,520: $63,429)

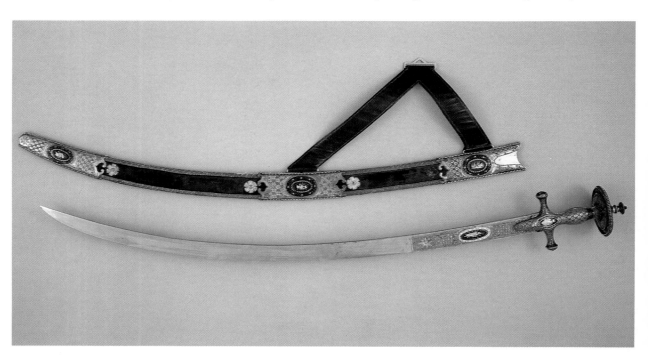

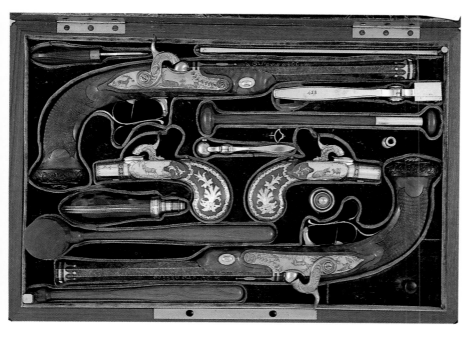

A cased set of French percussion duelling and pocket pistols, by Boutet, early 19th century, from the Draeger Collection, sold 7 December 1987.

PRICE
FF668,200 (£68,820: $122,890)

origin. It epitomizes the highest qualities of the armourer's and decorator's art. General Desaix had played an important role as administrator during the invasion of Egypt, and was known to local inhabitants as 'Le Sultan Juste'. The blade bears commemorative and personalized inscriptions on either side; on one it reads 'Affaire de Samaboud Conquete de la Haute Egypte', and on the other 'Le General Bonapart au General Desaix'.

If romance enhanced the appeal of some lots, technical brilliance was no less in evidence. Discerning collectors of French arms found a group of pistols by the renowned French maker Boutet of considerable interest. One pair in exceptional condition, complete with accessories in their rosewood case, secured the highest price in this remarkable sale.

COSTUME SALES

Part of the excitement of the auction world is that it is forever changing. Although Sotheby's first sold costume as early as 1967, it was material from Diaghilev's Ballets Russes that first set the market alight. Eighteenth-century dress, both male and female, was sold in a small way in furniture and works of art sales until a specialist department was set up at Sotheby's Belgravia in 1978. Since then the whole market has dramatically increased with museums and private collectors worldwide in hot competition. In some areas, such as eighteenth-century costume and twentieth-century couture, prices have risen by a remarkable 500 per cent.

Museums are the main buyers for the earlier periods and provenance can play an important part in achieving a high price. For example, a dove-grey silk Quaker wedding dress came with a copy of the original 1829 marriage certificate, which contributed to the price of £1,500. The pair of brown velvet breeches and matching coat worn by William James of Kent in 1751 as Black Rod of Ireland fetched £13,750. Here again the provenance probably added some 400 per cent to the result. The Devereux bodice, *c.* 1610, came not only with a complete history, but was also a stunning example of early needlework. The silver ground was worked in coloured silks with three-

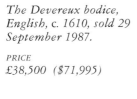

The Devereux bodice, English, c. 1610, sold 29 September 1987.

PRICE
£38,500 ($71,995)

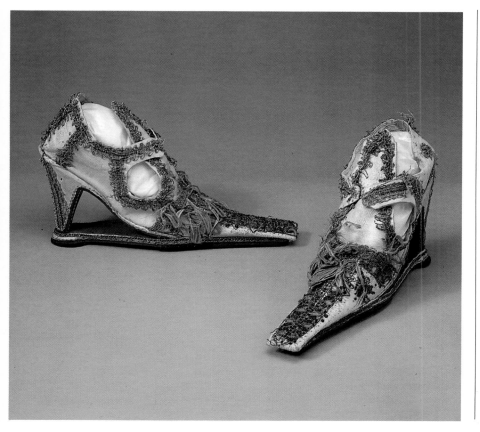

Above left. *Cut-velvet coat and breeches worn by the Black Rod of Ireland, William James of Kent, 1751, sold 9 May 1985.*

PRICE
£13,750 ($22,825)

Above right. *A plaid taffeta silk gown, c. 1860, sold 23 September 1986.*

PRICE
£2,420 ($3,945)

Left. *A pair of 'slap soled' shoes, Italian, c. 1630–60, sold 29 September 1987.*

PRICE
£20,900 ($34,067)

A blouse worn by Marilyn Monroe in the film Bus Stop, *sold 11 February 1988.*

PRICE
£7,050 ($12,000)

dimensional stump-work blooms and insects; the pea-pods even contained individually worked miniature peas. The bodice fetched £38,500.

While museums must try to assemble as complete a cross-section as possible of the history of costume, they are also well aware of their need to pull in the crowds. Black and sombre colours make for a dull display and are often, therefore, difficult to sell. The more brightly coloured the better, as is shown by the tartan silk gown, woven in bright primary colours, pictured on the previous page. It came with day and evening bodices and was also in excellent condition.

Condition is a major factor in determining price. Fashions are short-lived and dresses were frequently altered as taste or the wearer changed shape. Where the original fabric is uncut, but the costume is re-sewn or with a piece let in, then a rescue operation is possible without too great a fall in price. Once there is loss of fabric the value is radically reduced. Stains and fragile fabric will also reduce value at auction.

French *haute couture* up to the 1960s has proved an exceptionally strong seller recently. The names on the internationally fashion roll of honour:

Poiret, Fath, Molyneux, Schiaparelli, Balenciaga, Paquin, Patou, Lanvin, Dior and Coco Chanel make regular appearances at Sotheby's; Chanel was the subject of an exhibition last September. As the sculptural qualities of many of the modern designers are of paramount importance, alterations here will destroy most of the value. Survivors can achieve remarkable prices: in October last year a Jacques Fath black sheath gown of the late 1940s sold for £4,400 – an exception to the 'black is bad' rule.

As with earlier costume a link with a great name will transform a mundane article into a star performer and there is, perhaps, no greater star than Marilyn Monroe. The sale of her emerald-green satin, black net-trimmed, be-sequinned and fringed show-girl outfit from the 1956 hit film *Bus Stop* had all the makings of a media event. Sotheby's had it modelled during the sale by a Marilyn look-alike and it was sold to a New York businessman for his private collection for £15,950. A blouse worn by Monroe in the film made £7,050.

Kerry Taylor, who runs Sotheby's costume and textile department, makes many discoveries in the course of a year. On a visit to value a religious embroidery in a country house in Worcestershire, she asked if there were any costumes or dresses in the house. The owner thought her somewhat eccentric when she asked to be allowed to see the dressing-up box in her sons' bedroom. A photograph from the 1920s existed with the family wearing much of the contents. They were subsequently sold and among the many extraordinary treasures it contained were an embroidered hat from about 1700 (£1,600) and a shocking-pink eighteenth-century man's casual robe (£3,800). The boys lost their dressing-up box, but it fetched around £30,000.

A SPORTING PRINCE

On 9 January 1931, after lunching with his parents, George V and Queen Mary, the Prince of Wales visited Churchill's to order a pair of 'Premiere Quality' guns, numbers 4131/2. A day later, while hunting in Leicestershire, the Prince was introduced to Wallis Simpson at a house party given by Lady Furness in Melton Mowbray.

The guns were finished within five days, although such a pair usually took two years to complete, and the urgency suggests that the Prince had ordered them for the trip he was to take, on 16 January, to Central America with his brother Bertie, later George VI. The price they fetched set a world record for a pair of English 'side-by-side' game guns.

Right. *The Duke and Duchess of Windsor, with the Count de Chambrure and a loader, shooting in Alsace, 1951.*

Below. *One of the pair of 'Premiere Quality' XXV 12-bore sporting guns built by E.J. Churchill for Edward, Prince of Wales, 1931, sold 31 August 1987.*

PRICE
£42,900 ($68,640)

THE ROYAL BUICKS

This car was specially built by the Canadian McLaughlin-Buick plant to the order of King Edward VIII, then Prince of Wales. In August 1935, the Prince and Mrs Simpson went on a trip to their 'lovely villa *in the water*' in the South of France. Just before they left, the Prince paid a visit to Lendrum and Hartman Ltd, the concessionaires for Buick, at their showrooms in Albemarle Street.

Apparently, the company's senior director Captain Hartman was roused from his shaving chair at his barber's a few doors away to learn that the Prince of Wales wished to purchase two Buicks, one for himself, the other for 'a friend'. The friend was, of course, Mrs Simpson. A colleague was dispatched to the Buick factory in Canada, with orders not to return until the vehicles were complete. About a month after George V's death on 20 January 1936, they duly arrived in England. The King's model was registered CUL 421 and Mrs Simpson's CUL 547.

The 1936 Buick 37.8 hp DA90 'Limited' Limousine, with coachwork by McLaughlin of Oshawa, Canada, parked outside Sotheby's before the sale on 22 June 1987.

PRICE
£143,000 ($233,090)

TIFFANY SILVER AND GOLD

Today the Tiffany name is synonymous both with the finest silver and jewellery and with the Art Nouveau movement in the United States, but the two facets of this reputation developed almost entirely independently in the late nineteenth century. The firm Tiffany & Co., founded by Charles L. Tiffany as Tiffany & Young in 1837, prospered as a purveyor of elaborately wrought silver flatware and holloware to the industrialists of the Gilded Age and first achieved international recognition at the Paris Exposition in 1867. Tiffany designs included custom flatware for the Hearsts and the Vanderbilts, massive trophies for yacht clubs and racing associations, and elaborate presentation pieces such as the Bryant vase honouring the poet William Cullen Bryant, which is now in the Metropolitan Museum of Art in New York.

Charles Tiffany's son Louis Comfort Tiffany, on the other hand, followed a separate path, studying painting in Paris and ultimately choosing to express his artistic ideas in glass. His successful design for the Veteran's Room at the Seventh Regiment Armory in New York brought him many interior design commissions, and his windows, lamps, and other decorative objects, executed in the patent Favrile glass – a type of hand-made iridescent glass – by Tiffany Studios, became an integral part of the decor in fashionable houses.

There was little connection between Tiffany & Co. and Tiffany Studios until after Charles Tiffany's death in 1901. Shortly thereafter, L.C. Tiffany became design director at Tiffany & Co., and his influence can be seen in a number of pieces produced in the decades just before the first World War.

The year 1987 was the 150th anniversary of the founding of Tiffany & Co., and this event coincided with the sale last June of some magnificent pieces. These included a spectacular pair of candelabra on torchère stands, nearly six feet tall, made by Tiffany & Co., in 1884. By that time, silver was well established as a mark of affluence in America, and it is easy to imagine these candelabra flanking a fireplace or a doorway in one of the Newport 'cottages' or the mansions on the North Shore of Long Island. In style and in scale they capture the exuberant spirit of the era, when nothing was too big or too ornate. The Tiffany silversmith's mastery of his craft is clearly demonstrated in the skilful combination of relief and chased ornament incorporating a profusion of traditional decorative elements – acanthus, poppies, caryatids, classical borders, massive paw feet – with the firm's own chrysanthemum motif. Introduced on flatware in 1880, the shaggy chrysanthemum flower and foliage became one of Tiffany's most popular designs.

The candelabra are monogrammed 'MJM' for Mary Jane Morgan, wife of Charles Morgan, owner of Morgan's Louisiana and Texas Railroad and Steamship Company. She is said to have spent more than $4 million on her art collection, including a rumoured $24,000 to $40,000 for the candelabra. After her death in 1886, the entire collection was dispersed in a marathon three-day sale conducted by the American Art Association, one of Sotheby's predecessors in New York, and the candelabra fetched $8,100. In last year's

Sotheby's sale, on 24 June 1987, the price was $440,000.

In 1914, thirty years after the candelabra, Tiffany & Co. produced an exquisite gold box inset with enamelled cartouches and jewels. It was made during Louis Comfort Tiffany's time as design director and strongly reflects his influence. The four cartouches, each depicting a season, repeat the motifs of the famous *Four Seasons* stained glass panel. This panel was shown at the Paris Exposition of 1900, where L.C. Tiffany won a Grand Prix and five gold medals, and was subsequently installed in Laurelton Hall, his estate in Cold Spring Harbor, New York. The cluster of cabochon opals, the stone *par excellence* of Art Nouveau jewellery design, recalls the designs of Tiffany Studios, which often featured enamel or semi-precious stones set in bronze; it is also reminiscent of the rich, pebbly surface found in the Tiffany glass itself. The box was entered on the firm's ledgers on 30 April 1914. There is no record of the original owner, but an American private collector bought it last June for $401,500.

The 150th anniversary was commemorated last year by a series of exhibitions of silver and jewels at major museums throughout the United States, including the Metropolitan Museum of Art in New York and the Boston Museum of Fine Arts. The latter was especially fitting since a small Tiffany silver pitcher presented to the Museum of Fine Arts in 1876 was the first decorative work of art ever acquired by an American museum for its permanent collection.

Tiffany & Co., a jewel-set and enamelled 18-carat gold box, with cloisonné enamel, cabochon opals, tourmalines, blue and pink sapphires, and chrysoprases, New York, 1914, width 14.3 cm, sold 12 June 1987.

PRICE
$401,500 (£246,319)

THE $9 MILLION DIAMOND

The bidding opened at $6 million for the largest D-colour internally flawless diamond ever offered at auction. Moments later, at $9,130,000, this magnificent stone became the most expensive jewel in the world. Nonetheless, the new owner, London dealer Laurence Graff, maintained that the price was reasonable for a stone of such perfection. 'It really is a ball of fire; it refracts the light in a thousand directions. We could never hope to find such a stone again,' he exclaimed.

The sale of this 85.91 carat diamond was the climax of two days of jewellery auctions, totalling $36.7 million, a world record for a various owner jewel sale and second only to that of the Duchess of Windsor's collection.

Magnificent pear-shaped diamond, D-colour, internally flawless, 85.91 carats, sold 19 April 1988.

PRICE
$9,130,000 (£4,856,383)

A DAY IN THE COUNTRY: HOUSE SALES

S ales on the premises combine all the delights of country house visiting with the excitement of an auction. Somehow works of art take on a fuller meaning in such a setting, with their history still around them. Little wonder then that the viewings for Sotheby's country house sales in September and October 1987 – at Wilsford Manor, Tyninghame, Château de Claydael and Mount Juliet – were full to overflowing. Torrential rain failed to dampen spirits at Wilsford, and at Cleydael access to the moated château had to be barred at times, to allow people in the house to disperse. Buyers arrived by every conceivable means of transport, including helicopter!

When Sotheby's was asked to sell the contents of Wilsford Manor, Wiltshire, after the death of its owner the Hon. Stephen Tennant in February 1987, their experts entered a time-warp; the house had remained virtually unchanged for twenty years. Stephen Tennant had taken to his bed in the 1960s and his world had contracted to one room. From the papers heaped on the floor and lying like snow on tables and bureaux, silver expert John Culme reconstructed Tennant's fascinating story for the catalogue. In the 1920s, as a rich, gifted and hypnotically photogenic young man, Tennant's life had been an endless flurry of fancy dress balls, first nights at the Ballets Russes and

Stephen Tennant on a Syrie Maugham day bed, photographed by Cecil Beaton in the study at Wilsford in April 1938.

'White and gold and silver luxury': the interior of Wilsford Manor.

trips to Europe with his friend, the poet Siegfried Sassoon. He numbered among his other friends Cecil Beaton (who photographed him endlessly), Rex Whistler, the Sitwells, William Walton and E.M. Forster. A talented artist, he transformed the dark-panelled Wilsford Manor, designed by Detmar Blow in seventeenth-century style, into a house of 'white & gold & silver luxury', overrun with shell-shaped furniture and rococo mirrors.

If Wilsford's splendours were a little dimmed by years of neglect by the time Sotheby's arrived, the house came back to life as staff tidied, cleaned and re-lit rooms. Flowers once again filled the alcoves, furniture was rearranged to match schemes shown in old photographs. Tennant's successive phases of decoration were easy to track because of the vast number of manuscripts found in the house; John Culme was able to footnote many lots in the catalogue with dates of purchase and Tennant's reaction to his possessions.

Research also proved that Tennant's reputation as a shallow 'Bright Young Thing' was unjustified and revealed a writer and artist of seriousness and sensitivity. It was however the pleasure-loving side of Stephen Tennant, the leading spirit of countless house parties, that was recalled by his friends at a lunch given at Wilsford by Sotheby's UK Chairman, Lord Gowrie, before the sale. Among the guests were Lord Norwich; Laura, Duchess of Marlborough; Loelia, Lady Lindsay (formerly Duchess of Westminster); and a lady who remembered Stephen Tennant borrowing her rouge! The house, described by one observer as 'like the inside of a pair of silk pyjamas', was also enjoyed on that occasion by a younger generation of creative people 'who never knew Stephen but who ought to have done', such as Nicholas Coleridge of *Harpers & Queen* and the artist Glyn Boyd Harte.

The lawns slope gracefully away from the house; consequently the marquee, where the sale was held after items had been viewed *in situ*, had to be built on a special scaffold. The lawns were mown and the thickets of bamboo around the manor cut back, revealing unexpected treasures: a satyr here, an urn there, and part of the Italian garden Tennant created to remind him of the Mediterranean. At the sale the statuary was eagerly acquired by modern gardeners, with a bust of Pan making £7,150 and a pair of stone dwarves £8,250.

A busload of journalists was driven down to explore the house and

The drawing room at Wilsford.

subsequent press coverage aroused wide public interest. The first day of viewing dawned exceedingly wet, but even pouring rain throughout four viewing days did not stop over 2,000 people from examining the eighteenth-century furniture, the marble columns, the rare books and Stephen Tennant's delightful drawings. Wheels became bogged in the muddy car park, but tempers were soothed by excellent catering – hot curries for cold October days. After viewing ended there was a day's interval before the sale, during which Sotheby's porters (snugly accommodated for the duration in Wilsford's nursery wing) removed all traces of muddy feet from carpets and stripped the house for occupation by its new owner. All lots to be sold were stacked in order in the marquee.

The sale attracted local buyers, people down from London, dealers and international telephone bids. To make things easier, because of a large number of new private buyers, bidding was by numbered paddles, instead of the traditional 'nod-wink-and-raised-catalogue' system. It was undoubtedly the association with Stephen Tennant that made the Wilsford sale so successful, totalling £1.4 million.

Photographs of Tennant by Cecil Beaton soared far beyond estimates, with a buyer paying £3,740 for a 1927 half-length, estimated at £1,000–1,500. Epstein's bronze of Tennant made £24,200. A toy monkey that had accompanied Tennant to Marseilles in 1939 sold for £330, with four other toys. In other cases, it was intrinsic rather than associational value that ensured a high price: a pair of porphyry columns, of great interest to decorators, made £33,000 against an estimate of £4,000! 'Am I a legend?' asked Stephen Tennant a little before he died. As they carried off the scallop-shell chairs and Chinese lacquer screens, it was clear that the buyers thought so, and each took away a part of it.

The other three house sales had their own distinct character. The sale at Tyninghame was a classic Scottish country house sale, one of the largest held,

Stephen Tennant with a bronze bust by Epstein, c. 1927.

PRICE
£24,200 ($41,140)

Tyninghame House, East Lothian, seat of the Earls of Haddington since 1628, with the sale marquee in the foreground.

The sale at Tyninghame.

realizing a net total of £3.5 million. A rambling red baronial edifice in East Lothian, Tyninghame was filled with high quality furniture, silver and pictures. Never before open to the public, it attracted viewers who were simply curious, as well as private and trade buyers competing to possess items which in some cases had not been on the market for over a hundred years. A mid-eighteenth century Dutch marquetry commode sold extremely well at £110,000. The silver fetched higher prices than those that would have been achieved in London, an indication that serious bidders were there in force: a silver-gilt dessert service by William Chawner, dated 1827, made £52,800, four times its upper estimate, a response to the excellent condition of the little-used pieces. Tyninghame's portraits, evoking the family history and political alliances of the Earls of Haddington, were in several cases superb works of art as well. Sir Thomas Lawrence's well-known portrait of *George Canning* made £159,500 and Allan Ramsay's delicate *Katherine, Countess of Morton* was bid to £60,500, a record for the artist. Service for James I brought the 1st Earl of Haddington to prominence and the King rewarded his subject with a jewel-encrusted royal likeness by John de Critz; this was bought by a private buyer for £105,600.

The inclusion of unusual decorative pieces contributed to the success of the sale at Mount Juliet, an elegant eighteenth-century house set in the Kilkenny countryside. A dealer paid I£33,000 for a Regency cut-glass and gilt-metal hanging light, the kind of furnishing that is important for the detail of a room, but which tends to survive only in undisturbed country-house interiors. A porphyry centrepiece, eighteenth-century with nineteenth-century gilt-bronze mounts in the form of dragons, was discovered dismantled in the cellar. Expertly reassembled, it sold for I£18,700. A handsome, flower-patterned Louis XV marquetry *table à écrire*, stamped BVRB for the famous maker Bernard van Risenburgh, fetched I£44,000.

Mount Juliet is the site of a famous stud and its sporting paintings sold well. Among the Flemish and Dutch masters collected by Mount Juliet's owners the McCalmonts, two bird pieces by Hondecoeter made I£181,500, more than doubling estimates. Again, the novelty of a house not open to the public attracted swarms of visitors, among them local tenants, who bore away

small lots of household goods ('four kitchen chairs ... two watering cans') as mementoes of the end of an era.

Over on the Continent Sotheby's staff, walled up in the moated Château Cleydael, enjoyed a taste of the Middle Ages for three weeks as they prepared for the company's first Belgian house sale. A siege by local antique dealers, who challenged Sotheby's right to hold the auction, brought a not unwelcome notoriety, and the spectacular setting of the fourteenth-century château did the rest. A mixture of house contents and other properties realized prices well above estimates. It seems that in both Britain and Europe house sales capture the public imagination.

Château de Claydael, Belgium.

AN UNUSUAL LALIQUE FIGURE

René Lalique, who is better known as a designer of exquisite jewellery and a glassmaker, probably modelled this extraordinary figure of a woman himself. Most of his later *cire perdue* works were executed from his sketches by other craftsmen in the Lalique factory. *Cire perdue*, literally translated, means 'lost wax': a mould is made round a wax model, and when molten glass or metal is poured in, the wax melts and is thus lost. The figure appears to be a companion piece to the figure of *La Grande Nue aux Cheveux Longs* in the collection of the Lalique family, which dates from *c.* 1901. This unusual work fetched $148,500, a record for the artist.

René Lalique, cire perdue Figure of a Woman, c. *1901–5, height of figure 44 cm, sold 21 November 1987.*

PRICE
$148,500 (£86,337)

MARY STRICKLER'S QUILT COLLECTION

Mary Strickler's Quilt Collection, assembled by Linda Reuther and Julie Silber of California, takes its name from a magnificent Mariner's Compass design, perfectly pieced and stitched and signed by Mary Royer Strickler of Bucks County, Pennsylvania, in 1834. The sale of this important collection in January 1988 was a great event for collectors of American folk art.

The growth of the Mary Strickler collection from the late 1960s onwards coincided with an increasing recognition of quilts both as historical documents and as expressions of artistic design. In 1971 the Whitney Museum of American Art exhibited a portion of the collection of Jonathan Holstein and Gail van der Hoof, displaying the quilts open on the walls and describing them in formal terms in the catalogue, thus conveying for the first time the aesthetic appeal of these domestic objects. Ten years later, another landmark exhibition, 'American Quilts: A Handmade Legacy', was mounted by the Oakland Museum. By being displayed alongside related objects, historical photographs and excerpts from letters and diaries, the quilts were

Album quilt for John and Rebecca Chamberlain, probably by Mary Evans, Baltimore, 1848, 2.74 by 2.74 m approx., sold 30 January 1988.

PRICE
$110,000 (£58,510)

Pieced silk and taffeta log cabin quilt, c. 1870, 1.83 by 1.83 m approx., sold 30 January 1988.

PRICE
$7,975 (£4,242)

reconnected to the lives of the women who had made them.

Quilting was a universal skill among eighteenth- and nineteenth-century American women, one that they acquired from their mothers at a very early age and practised throughout their lives. By the time a young woman was engaged, she was expected to have completed twelve quilts, and the thirteenth, her bridal quilt, fashioned of the best materials she could afford and with her most skilled needlework, was executed during her engagement.

Most quilts are the work of one woman. The well-known American quilting-bees were organized by the quiltmaker to gather neighbouring women to assist her only in the final phase, the stitching together of the colourful top design with the lining and the backing. Some others, such as album and presentation quilts, were collaborative efforts, but even with these each woman would make a separate square of her own fabric and design, and sign her name on it. Rarely are two quilts indentical. Within a basic pattern, the border, colour, fabric and quilting stitches were all varied for an individual effect. Women could express themselves creatively in quiltmaking and their finest work was carefully preserved and displayed only on special occasions.

The range of the quilter's art was well represented in the Mary Strickler collection. Undoubtedly the most spectacular piece was a rare Baltimore album quilt, made probably by Mary Evans for John and Rebecca Chamberlain. Baltimore album quilts, so called because of their elaborate and sometimes narrative appliqués making up a sort of 'album' of images, are extremely rare; indeed only fifty are known to exist. Twelve of these album quilts are known to be from the hand of Mary Evans, an exceptionally gifted professional seamstress and quiltmaker active in Baltimore in the 1840s and 1850s. She also made up appliquéd squares which she sold to other women and from time to time quilts are found containing one or more of these purchased sections. They are usually quite easy to distinguish, however, by their technical superiority. For this particular quilt, which was probably made to commemorate the Chamberlains' marriage, Evans used the finest cloth, much of it French and English printed material, which gave her the opportunity to model the flowers, fruits and birds she portrayed. This rare and important quilt was sold for $110,000.

Another album quilt, although dating from some forty years or more later, was an unusual embroidered and painted album/crazy quilt in silk, velvet and taffeta, inscribed 'S.J. Buell'. It has been surmised that this is connected with Sarah Buell Hale, the editor of *Godey's Lady's Book*, a magazine which advocated crowded and elaborate needlework. The quilt also exhibits an awareness of trends in the decorative arts of its day: included among the designs are oriental motifs – storks, fans, insects and the like – which are certainly inspired by the international Aesthetic movement, best exemplified in America by the silver produced by Tiffany during the last quarter of the nineteenth century. As with the Baltimore quilt, the sumptuous materials and the quality and complexity of design suggest an urban rather than a rural origin. In fact, the 'Buell Quilt' has been regarded by some as the 'quintessential Victorian quilt' with its bright colours, intricate needlework and highlighting with pigment. It sold for $26,400.

Pieced silk, velvet, taffeta and chenille 'Horse Crazy' quilt, initialled HMR (Helen Mary Rounsville), 1880–90, 1.64 by 1.30 m, sold 30 January 1988.

PRICE
$14,300 (£7,606)

Another quilt that did well, selling for $14,300 – more than twice its top estimate – was a highly original, almost bizarre, 'Horse Crazy' quilt. Made for Helen Mary Rounsville of Fowlersville, Michigan, by a member of her family, it successfully combines her dual interests in horses and gardening. Groups of flowers and plants – pansies, daisies, strawberries, wheat – were embroidered on irregularly shaped pieces of black silk, and this was surrounded by a border of red velvet appliquéd with palomino and black horses. The naïveté of design gives the quilt a special, and uniquely American, appeal.

A ROMAN DRINKING-CUP

Even in Roman times, this small drinking-cup, or *skyphos*, would have been considered a treasured possession, and was probably owned by a private collector. It is one of only about twelve cameo glasses to survive from the ancient world in near-perfect condition; others include the well-known Portland Vase in the British Museum. The rarity of cameo glass was then such that, if damaged, it was often repaired, as the Portland Vase has been.

'Cameo' is a term usually associated with gemstones, which cameo glass imitated. A low-relief design was set against a plane in a contrasting colour. Great technical virtuosity was called for in the making of the glass. Two layers of glass, blue and white, were bound together, and the figured design was produced by carving away the opaque white outer layer. This allowed for subtle mid-tones, as the translucent blue would permeate the thinner layers of white relief.

The *skyphos* is decorated with scenes of chariot racing, and there is such attention to detail that the charioteer's mode of dress is an interesting period document. His cloak, billowing in the wind, suggests movement, and despite the difficulty of working in such low relief the modelling is highly expressive.

A Roman dark blue cameo glass skyphos, *c. 25 BC–25 AD, 8.3 cm high (restored), 10.8 cm wide, sold 20 November 1987.*

PRICE
£352,000 ($665,280)

A VALUABLE CHINESE VASE

An outstanding example of Ming porcelain, this vase realized a world record for any Chinese work of art. Yet it was originally discovered by Sotheby's in Europe being used as a bedroom lamp! It sold through Sotheby's London in December 1980 for the then remarkable price of £319,000; the buyer on that occasion was Mr T.Y. Chao, one of the greatest recent collectors of Chinese art. When his collection was auctioned in turn – in Hong Kong on 19 May 1987 – the vase went for an astounding HK$11,220,000 (£864,407). The piece is especially notable for its glaze. Copper-red is difficult to fire correctly, and usually results in a greyish tone. The fine, pinkish-red colour here, however, is of top quality, and despite its domestic misuse the vase has remained in good condition for over six hundred years.

A Ming copper-red glazed vase, late 14th century, 31.5 cm high, from the T.Y. Chao private and family trust collections, sold 19 May 1987.

PRICE
HK$11,220,000 (£864,407: $1,438,462)

UNTITLED

Jackson Pollock, Untitled, c. *1948, oil and collage on paper mounted on masonite, 78.8 by 58.5 cm, sold 4 November 1987.*

PRICE
$1,210,000 (£703,488)

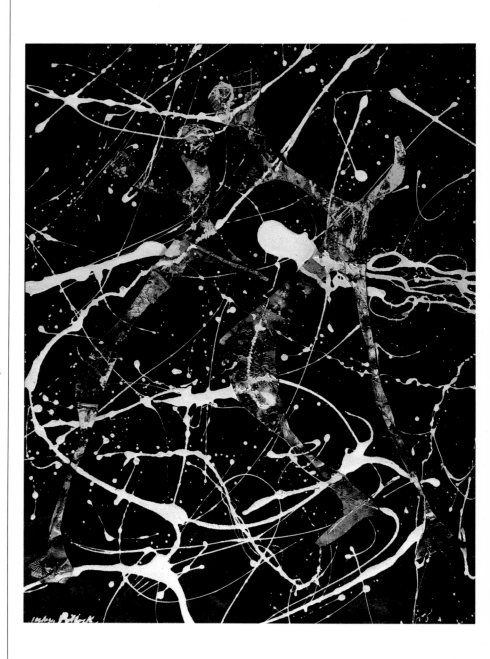

PINK LADY

Willem de Kooning, Pink Lady, c. *1944, oil and charcoal on panel, 122.5 by 89.5 cm, sold 4 May 1987.*

PRICE
$3,630,000 (£2,186,747)

DIAMONDS AT AUCTION

'He who purchases a diamond buys a fragment of eternity', observed a seventeenth-century Hindu philosopher. A gift of nature conceived more than four hundred million years ago, the diamond has extraordinary physical properties that have made it a symbol of wealth, power, and passion since antiquity.

Sotheby's involvement with the world's most important jewels began almost as soon as the firm was established nearly two and a half centuries ago. It was not until the 1960s, however, that the sales of great gemstones began to take off, with the spectacular prices realized at one sale completely eclipsed by the next.

The Taylor-Burton-Cartier diamond, a 69.4-carat pear-shape, was the first to break the million-dollar mark. The bidding for the stone in October 1969 was an electrifying duel between an agent for Richard Burton and Cartier, finally ending at $1.05 million. Victorious in the saleroom, Cartier resold the diamond to Mr Burton the next day and he presented it to Elizabeth Taylor.

The world record price for a jewel, $9,130,000, was paid in April 1988 for a magnificent pear-shaped, D-colour, flawless stone weighing 85.91 carats,

The Porter Rhodes Diamond, square emerald-cut diamond weighing 54.99 carats, flanked by 6 baguette diamonds, within a platinum mounting, by Harry Winston, sold 20 October 1987.

PRICE
$3,850,000 (£2,319,277)

The Jonker No. 4
Diamond, emerald-cut
diamond weighing 30.70
carats, flanked by 2 tapered
baguette diamonds, within
a platinum ring mounting,
by Harry Winston, sold 8
December 1987.

PRICE
$1,705,000 (£931,694)

the largest of its type ever to be offered at auction (see page 61).

Last autumn, two more remarkable diamonds, both with a prominent place in the history of diamond collecting, were sold in New York. The Porter Rhodes Diamond, discovered on 12 February 1880 on the Rhodes claim at the Kimberley Mine, is a stone of exceptional colour and clarity, the first of such quality to be found in South Africa.

The 153.50-carat octahedron was first exhibited uncut at the Bond Street Museum of Edwin Streeter, and the Colonel in charge of the Crown Jewels arranged an audience for Porter Rhodes with Queen Victoria, then in residence at Osborne House on the Isle of Wight. Both she and Empress Eugenie were quick to recognize its beauty, but they doubted whether it could have come from the Cape. At that time, brilliant whiteness was synonymous with an Indian or Brazilian origin and stones from South Africa were dismissed as inferior.

The diamond has since passed through several different hands; once the wedding gift of the Duke of Westminster to his wife, it was later acquired for the collection of the Maharaja of Indore. Now mounted as a ring in an elegant setting by Harry Winston, the Porter Rhodes was bought by the London dealer Laurence Graff for $3,850,000 in October 1987.

A second famous South African stone, the Jonker No. 4 Diamond, made the highest price – $1,705,000 – in a sale in December 1987. This 30.70-carat stone was one of thirteen cleaved from the enormous 726-carat diamond discovered on the claim of Johannes Jacobus Jonker, an impoverished prospector, in 1935. To ensure its safety, Mrs Jonker hung the diamond around her neck and was protected by armed guards until it could be sold. The diamond was then mailed to London (registered, of course!) and resold to

Shirley Temple holding the Jonker Diamond before it was cut.

Harry Winston, who exhibited it there during the celebrations for George V's Silver Jubilee and at the American Museum of Natural History in New York.

Ultimately, however, the Jonker was cut by Lazare Kaplan, a man from a long line of Belgian diamond-cutters and one of the best and most flamboyant of his day. He and Winston spent more than a year studying its structure before the attempt. Other lapidaries estimated the chances at less than fifty per cent and Lloyd's declined to insure the Jonker against damage. In the end, Kaplan's calculations were correct, and the perfectly cleaved stone yielded the 125-carat Jonker No. 1 and a dozen smaller stones. The magnificent Jonker No. 1, considered by many to be the most perfectly cut diamond in the world, has been owned by King Farouk and Queen Ratna of Nepal and is now in a private collection. The other Jonker diamonds were also avidly purchased by illustrious names including the Maharaja of Indore, who is reputed to have bought four, and John D. Rockefeller. The Jonker No. 4 is now in a private American collection.

WHY CHOOSE BLUE?

Thi**s painting, *IKB 74*, achieved a record price for the artist, Yves Kline, when it was sold in London recently. The artist was often asked why he had chosen the colour blue. In reply he quoted from Gaston Bachelard's *Air and Dreams*, in which Bachelard describes an 'excessively hostile blueness' which strives with an 'indefatigable hand' to 'fill the gaping blue holes wickedly made by birds'. Kline commented on this:

> In the realm of the blue air more than anywhere else one feels that the world is accessible to the most unlimited reverie. It is then that a reverie assumes true depth. The blue sky yawns beneath the dreams, the dream escapes from the two-dimensional image; soon in a paradoxical way the airborne dream exists only in depth, while the two other dimensions, in which picturesque and painted reverie are entertained, lose all visionary interest. The world is thus on the far side of an unsilvered mirror, there is an imaginary beyond, a beyond pure and insubstantial, and that is the dwelling place of Bachelard's beautiful phrase: 'First there is nothing, next there is a depth of nothingness, then a profundity of blue.'
>
> Blue has no dimensions, it is beyond dimensions, whereas the other colours are not. They are pre-psychological expanses, red, for example, presupposing a site radiating heat. All colours arouse specific associative ideas, psychologically material or tangible, while blue suggests at most the sea and sky, and they, after all, are in actual, visible nature what is most abstract.

(Yves Klein, extract from a lecture at the Sorbonne, 1959)

Yves Klein, IKB 74, 1958, blue pigment in synthetic resin on fabric laid down on panel, 200 by 140 cm, sold 2 July 1987.

PRICE
£638,000 ($1,049,510)

ROCK AND ROLL SALES

From Old Masters to old electric guitars might seem an unlikely spread of markets for a fine art auction house, but Sotheby's Rock and Roll sales are now very much a part of the auction scene.

The first sale, held in December 1981, was a fairly tentative experiment: it all began with a couple of upright pianos belonging to Elton John too modern to fit into a sale of antique instruments. But the idea of a sale of music memorabilia caught the imagination of the national and local press and the advance coverage that the sale received brought items flooding in from individuals all over the country.

On the morning of that sale, the hysteria outside the saleroom was astonishing: the Beatles' first manager, who was there, compared it to pre-concert Beatlemania. When the doors opened there was a rush for seats and within the first five minutes all were taken; even standing room was full. A new annual event had been staged, and these auctions in the UK and USA have since generated a healthy £3 million.

Most of the big names have featured in our Rock and Roll sales: Elvis Presley, Buddy Holly, Eddie Cochran, the Beatles, the Rolling Stones, the Who, Cream, Jimi Hendrix, Pink Floyd, David Bowie, T. Rex and the Sex Pistols. Teenagers too young to have seen the groups themselves vie with fans in their thirties or forties and parents on present-buying sprees. Lots range from album-cover artwork, recordings of unreleased songs, manuscript lyrics of well-known songs, stage and film costume, musical instruments, letters, presentation discs and awards, photographs and even cars.

Particular highlights have included lyrics for 'Imagine', 'Gimme Some Truth', 'It's Only Love', 'One Thing You Can't Hide', and 'I'm in Love' – the last, written in Lennon's own handwriting, was never actually recorded by the Beatles but by the Fourmost, to whom the handwritten lyrics were given. Lyrics by Mark Feld (Marc Bolan) for 'Metal Guru' and by Phil Collins for 'If Leaving Me Is Easy' also proved to be coveted – and expensive – prizes.

The actual costumes worn by singers during concerts or in films are often the most hotly contested items – there have been stage suits worn by members of the Beatles in concert, in album cover photographs and in the film *A Hard Day's Night*, as well as outfits worn by Elvis Presley, Mick Jagger and Jimi Hendrix. Some remarkable instruments have also come under the hammer: John Lennon's electric guitar, an acoustic guitar belonging to George Harrison, a bass guitar that belonged to Stuart Sutcliffe (the original fifth member of the Beatles), several of Jimi Hendrix's guitars, a Cat Stevens acoustic guitar, and drum kits used by Ginger Baker, Mitch Mitchell and Carl Palmer.

Although lyrics, costumes and instruments tend to be owned by people who had close contacts with the musicians, the majority of the lots included in the auctions are brought in by members of the public who were fans at the time and hunted autographs at concerts or by post. Previously unknown photographs of musicians in the early stages of their careers have often been

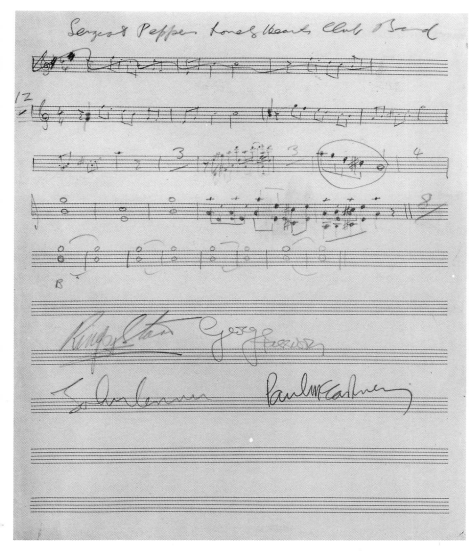

The original manuscript horn orchestration for 'Sergeant Pepper's Lonely Hearts Club Band', 1967, signed by all four members of the Beatles, 20 by 25 cm, sold 5 August 1987.

PRICE
£5,280 ($8,395)

John Entwistle's red suede and yellow leather flame motif stage costume with matching Peter Cook customized Fender electric bass guitar, early 1970s, sold 7 April 1988.

PRICE
costume £4,030 ($6,408); guitar £16,500 ($30,855)

dug out of attics by people who are amazed to learn that they could be worth hundreds of pounds.

The Rock and Roll auctions are now important international events: seats are reserved for collectors from America, Japan and Australia, and on an important lot three or four overseas bidders may be competing by telephone. In the sale room, beneath the lights of television camera crews, the flash bulbs from the world's press erupt as a record price is made. But most of the buyers remain the fans and the young, and it is still possible to take away your own little corner of music history – a letter or a signed album cover – for a few pounds.

EINSTEIN AT WORK

This extraordinary document, Einstein's fullest treatment of the Special Theory of Relativity, was purchased last December by an anonymous collector for $1,155,000, a record for a manuscript sold in America. Commenting on its importance, the new owner expressed his belief that the manuscript 'represents the highest intellectual achievement of our century, which can only be placed along with that of Aristotle, Leonardo and Newton'. Commissioned in 1912 for the fifth volume of Erich Marx's *Handbuch der Radiologie*, but never published, the 72-page article is the longest of Einstein's discussions of his revolutionary theory. As a working scientific manuscript, it is full of emendations and references; even the famous equation E = mc² is reconsidered.

Albert Einstein, 'On the Theory of Relativity', Prague or Zurich, 1912 (?), 72 leaves, small folio, 36 by 22.5 cm, sold 2 December 1987.

PRICE
$1,155,000 (£631,148)

JOHN GOULD, THE BIRD MAN

On 23 April 1987 Sotheby's offered for sale John Gould's own collection of his famous bird books, described in his will as his 'private library copy', containing a total of 3,265 hand-coloured lithographed plates. The thirteen works in rich green morocco bindings were housed in a handsome walnut-veneered cabinet commissioned by Gould and had remained undisturbed since his death over a hundred years ago, passing down through the family to Gould's great-grandson, Dr Geoffrey Edelsten. Complete sets of Gould's books are extremely rare, and the fact that these were also his own personal copies made them uniquely attractive to collectors.

John Gould (1804–1881) was born at Lyme Regis in Dorset, and shortly afterwards moved to Stoke Hill, near Guildford. He first worked under his father as a gardener at Windsor Castle, and later at Ripley Castle, and it was probably the outdoor occupation that stimulated an interest in birds. This enthusiasm led him at first towards taxidermy: most of his subjects in this field were birds, but intriguingly, one of his largest commissions was a giraffe belonging to George IV. Gould's career was given a fillip in 1827 when he was appointed 'Curator Preserver' of the collection of the Zoological Society of London. Soon after this, he acquired for the Society a valuable collection of bird skins from the Himalayas and, while working on their preservation, had the idea of recording bird species in book form. Thus began the publication of his extensive series of magnificently illustrated folio volumes. These include (in chronological order): *The Birds of Europe, The Birds of Australia, The Mammals of Australia, A Monograph of the Trochilidae or Family of Humming-Birds, The Birds of Asia, The Birds of Great Britain* and *The Birds of New Guinea*; in addition he produced monographs on the

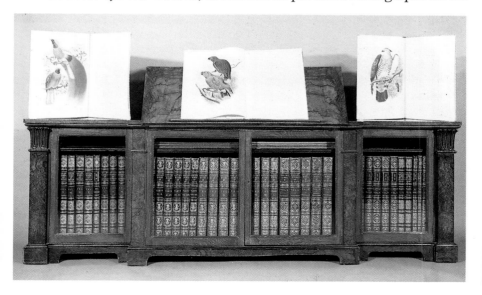

John Gould's own copies of his celebrated bird books, 1831–88, 13 works, sold 23 April 1987.

PRICE
£397,485 ($683,674)

toucans of the tropical forests of America, the vividly coloured trogons ('denizens of the intertropical regions of the Old and New World' as he called them), and the partridges of America. As if all this was not a lifetime's work in itself, Gould also found time for over three hundred scientific articles and several smaller books. In 1843 he was elected a Fellow of the Royal Society and many other honours followed from learned bodies throughout the world. As the leading British ornithologist of his day he was the recognized authority on the birds of Australia, and with the help of collectors and other ornithologists discovered hundreds of previously unknown species.

Although Gould himself did not execute finished drawings for any of his works, he did provide rough pencil or watercolour sketches with notes for his

Eagle Owl from The Birds of Europe, *sold 23 April 1987.*

PRICE
£35,200 ($60,544)

EAGLE OWL.
Bubo maximus (Sibbald)

artists to work from, and he was the moving spirit behind the grand conception of the plates. The accomplished artists who transformed the sketches into watercolour drawings and then transferred them onto lithographic stones, included his wife Elizabeth, Edward Lear, Joseph Wolf, Henry Richter and William Hart, the most outstanding being Lear and Wolf. The new technique of lithography introduced a greater freedom of line and softer tones than had hitherto been known, and was ideally suited as a medium for bird pictures. The finished prints resembled watercolours, with the birds set in their natural habitats often amongst plants and flowers. Gould was meticulous about accuracy, both in design and colouring, and his personal set of the works was coloured to the highest standard.

Culmenated Toucans from A Monograph of the Ramphastidae, or Family of Toucans, *sold 23 April 1987.*

PRICE *£6,600 ($11,352)*

CHINESE BRONZE ZODIAC FIGURES

Below. *Head of a monkey and a boar, c. 1750, bronze, heights 48.3cm and 32.4cm, sold 9 October 1987.*

PRICE
monkey $165,000 (£101,226); boar $104,500 (£64,110)

Below right. *Detail from an engraving in* The palaces, pavilions and gardens ... in the grounds of the Yuan Ming Yuan.

PRICE
$55,000 (£33,742)

These two bronze animal heads, a monkey and a boar, were once part of a magnificent horological fountain in the grounds of the Yuan Ming Yuan, the European-style Summer Palace of Emperor Qianlong (1738–95), near Beijing. Twelve bronze animals representing the signs of the Chinese zodiac were incorporated into a huge stone shell fountain known as the 'Palace of the Calm Sea'. Water flowed from each figure in turn, and at noon and midnight all worked in unison. Twenty engravings of the palace complex were commissioned by Emperor Qianlong and a reprint of this set was offered in the same sale as the two zodiac heads. The illustrated plate shows part of the fountain with zodiac figures and the building which housed the waterworks. The monkey brought $165,000 and the boar fetched $104,500.

AN EGYPTIAN GODDESS IN STONE

This statue once stood among more than six hundred figures of Sekhmet, goddess of war and protector of the king, which adorned the courts and passageways of the great temple that Amenhotep III built in honour of the goddess Mut at Thebes. It probably came originally from the temple of King Amenophis III in western Thebes. Amenophis was described as 'beloved of Sekhmet, mistress of the goddesses'.

Figure of the goddess Sekhmet, Thebes, 18th Dynasty, 1403–1365 BC, diorite, height 109.2 cm, sold 24 November 1987.

PRICE
$495,000 (£279,661)

THE DE BELDER LIBRARY

The de Belder sale.

'Good evening. Tonight we are selling books from the celebrated botanical library of Robert de Belder.

Lot 1 [pre-sale estimate £1,800–2,000]. £1,500 for this? Thank you sir, £1,800, £2,000, £2,500, £3,000, £4,000 ... £11,000, £12,000, £13,000, £14,000, £15,000. All done? At £15,000 then.' The hammer fell and the purchaser's name – Hirsch – was called out. It was said afterwards that at this point several dealers multiplied their bids for the whole sale.

Thus the scene was set for what was to prove to be the greatest colour-plate botanical book sale of all time. Estimated to make under £3 million, the sale made nearly £6 million.

Robert de Belder, the collector of the library, a retired Belgian diamond dealer, had both knowledge and means. He also had and took every opportunity to secure the finest copies from many of the finest collections. Single-mindedly, he created the greatest private collection of botanical books in the world. The 388 lots in the sale represented one-tenth of the library in volume but included all the greatest monuments of botanical illustration from 1600 to 1900; it thus documented the whole evolution of botanical art.

A Vice-President of the Royal Horticultural Society, Robert de Belder had purchased the Arboretum Kalmthout, situated on a 22-acre site 15 miles north of Antwerp, in 1952. Originally founded by Charles Van Geart in the nineteenth century, which was a golden age for horticulture in Belgium, it had been in a process of decay since the 1930s. The de Belders took up permanent residence at Kalmthout and restored the Arboretum; it is now a conspicuous feature of the European horticultural landscape. One of the charms of the garden is that it was not designed on paper, but developed around existing elements. There are flowers all the year round. Over one hundred students have trained at Kalmthout, working closely with the permanent staff. The library was collected as a reference tool of its living adjunct, the Arboretum, and the books had a direct relevance to the development of the botanical garden.

Mr de Belder's taste, judgement and skill in acquiring great copies of great books was more than fully justified at the sale. His copy of Basil Besler's *Hortus Eystettensis*, printed in 1613, was probably the finest in existence of one of the greatest flower books ever produced. It is the first great florilegium 'splendid in its array of large drawings, magnificent as a record of the plants in a German garden at the beginning of the seventeenth century'. Divided into four sections, one for each season, the work commemorates the celebrated gardens of its patron, Johann Konrad von Gemmingen, Prince Bishop of Eichstätt.

The plates depict over 1,000 flowers, representing 667 species. Sadly, the

Lilium Cruentum Polyanthos *from Basil Besler,* Hortus Eystettensis, *1613, 54.0-55.0 by 41.0 cm, sold 27 April 1987.*

PRICE
£605,000 ($974,050)

Opposite. Night-blowing
Cereus *from Robert
Thornton,* The Temple of
Flora, *[1799–]1807, sold 27
April 1988.*

PRICE
£187,000 ($353,430)

Bishop's garden was not long to outlast his death: with the outbreak of the Thirty Years War six years later, it deteriorated and by 1633 the celebrated collection of plants had become a vegetable plot. When this copy of the book was bought in 1981 it had cost £90,200. On 27 April 1987 it realized £605,000.

One of the most memorable – and tense – moments in bookselling history came with lot 362, Trew's *Hortus Nitidissimis* (1750–86), among the most sumptuous and most elusive flower books. Few complete copies are known, partly due to the fact that it was published over a 36-year period. It is no exaggeration to say that the collective breaths of the audience were held – punctuated by outbursts of nervous laughter as the bidders were encouraged by the auctioneer to make yet another bid even though they had repeatedly admitted defeat. The bidding mounted from £12,000 and extended over nearly 5 whole minutes, an eternity in the saleroom. The battle was fought primarily between Nico Israel, the Dutch dealer in the room, doubtless representing a private collector, and the mysterious buyer, who had wanted to leave a fixed bid but had been persuaded by a member of staff to participate in person over the telephone. The pre-sale estimate was £50,000–60,000. The hammer fell at £280,000.

Another item deserves special mention: de Belder's copy of the most famous English botanical plate book, Robert Thornton's *New Illustration of the Sexual System of Carolus von Linnaeus* – incorporating the splendid 'Temple of Flora' – which was printed between 1799 and 1807. The copy in this sale was exceptional and made the exceptional price of £187,000, upwards of £100,000 more than any previous copy.

Thornton intended the work as a pictorial celebration, accompanied by prose and verse text, of Linnaeus' treatise on the reproduction of plants. He employed the artists Peter Henderson, Philip Reinagle, and others to paint the plants, each in an exotic and romantic setting. Abraham Pether contributed the 'moon-light' accompanying the plate of the night-blowing cereus. Sydenham Edwards painted the hyacinths, and Thornton himself painted the rose. The mezzotint engraving was done by Ward, Earlom and Dunkarton, and the acquatint engraving by Stadler and Sutherland. Thornton exhausted his fortune on the book's production, with the result that he had to petition Parliament to conduct a lottery in order to avoid bankruptcy. He blamed his failure to secure sufficient subscribers for his book on war, and wrote bitterly 'The once *moderately rich* very justly now complain that they are exhausted through *Taxes* laid on them to pay armed men to diffuse *rapine, fire,* and *murder,* over *civilized* EUROPE.'

Any account of the de Belder library would be incomplete without mention of the work of the Belgian painter Pierre-Joseph Redouté, 1759–1840. He survived the great upheavals of French politics, producing an unrivalled sequence of colour-plate illustrations utilizing the technique of stipple engraving. Among his students and patrons were five queens and empresses of France, as well as the celebrated Duchesse de Berry. The de Belder collection included incomparable copies of Redouté's *Les Liliacées* and *Les Roses,* the latter being inscribed by him: 'Cette exemplaire est un des premier tirage et des plus beaux – Redouté.' *Les Liliacées* was Redouté's largest and most ambitious work and is generally regarded as his masterpiece. Only 200 copies of the book were printed and it was produced under the patronage of the Empress Josephine. Both works made exceptional prices: *Les Roses* £143,000 and *Les Liliacées* £154,000, both considerably more than any previous copies. The original drawings for *Les Liliacées* were auctioned by Sotheby's in New York in 1985 for $5,500,000.

The Flower by Reinagle. Moonlight by Pether.   Caldwall sculp.

The Night-Blowing Cereus

A PAIR OF BOULLE PEDESTALS

This magnificent pair of Louis XIV ormolu-mounted brass and tortoiseshell-inlaid ebony pedestal cabinets, attributed to the ébéniste André-Charles Boulle, was once part of the famous collection of the tenth Duke of Hamilton (1767–1852). In 1882, the Duke's possessions were sold in what was one of the most important auctions of French furniture ever to have taken place. The pedestals were illustrated in the catalogue for this sale, and their provenance has been traced even further back to the 1827 auction of the collection of the Chevalier Féréol Bonnemaison, an artist and restorer who had previously acted as an intermediary between the Duke and the artist Jacques-Louis David. Charles Boulle never signed his furniture and the attribution to him must remain tentative, but the high quality of craftsmanship together with stylistic features lead to the conclusion that the pedestals are indeed his work.

A pair of Louis XIV ormolu-mounted brass and tortoiseshell ebony pedestal cabinets, c. 1710, attributed to André-Charles Boulle, sold 31 October 1987.

PRICE
$990,000 (£607,362)

A CARTIER EPAULETTE

This is perhaps the most important jewel by Cartier ever to be auctioned by Sotheby's in London. The inspiration behind it is probably the Indian *turah*, or turban ornament, often translated to a long tassel, which inspired many of Cartier's designs during the 1920s. Surviving epaulettes are extremely rare and are among the most distinctive and sensational jewels of the period, worn attached to the shoulder of a dress.

The drop of the present piece is designed as a large stylized iris motif, set with diamonds and emeralds. Two of the three emerald drops are of Indian workmanship and probably date from the turn of the century.

Cartier, Paris, an emerald and diamond epaulette, c. 1920, sold 24 March 1988.

PRICE
£231,000 ($408,870)

GERMAN PAINTING SALES IN MUNICH

Although much of the art market is international, there are also local, specialized markets. For example, for some years Sotheby's has been holding sales of Swiss furniture and paintings in Zurich, attracting an enthusiastic, chiefly Swiss, group of buyers. Often schools of art which originally appealed mainly to the nation which produced them are critically re-evaluated and begin to attract international demand. This has recently happened with turn-of-the-century Scandinavian painting and twentieth-century Scottish Colourists. American collectors who a decade ago might not have heard of Hammershøi or Zorn, now value them for painterly qualities akin to Sargent and Whistler. The Scottish Colourists' debt to Impressionism and Post-Impressionism has enticed Impressionist collectors to buy Colourist work as they discover stylish and original art at a fraction of Impressionist prices.

There has long existed an international market for German painting; but Sotheby's decision to hold twice-yearly sales of nineteenth and twentieth-century German art in Munich was for the convenience of the large number of collectors in Germany itself. German collectors respond strongly to all periods of their country's art, and interest in the arts is at a high level: almost every exhibition and sale preview at Sotheby's is packed with people.

Hermann Max Pechstein, Rettungsboot, *1911, oil on canvas, 70 by 80 cm, sold 11 November 1987.*

PRICE
DM423,500 (£140,464: $244,798)

Erich Heckel, Cabaret Szene, *coloured crayons and pen and ink, 9 by 14 cm, sold 11 November 1987.*

PRICE
DM38,500 (£12,790: $22,254)

German eighteenth- and nineteenth-century painting is still not very well known internationally, partly because the largest holdings are still in Germany. Even artists with international reputations, like Caspar David Friedrich, are extremely rare outside Germany: a handful of his paintings are in American museums, only one in a British public collection. By contrast, American museums abound in fine works by Expressionist and *Neue Sachlichkeit* artists – art which was considered degenerate by the Nazis and was taken to America by refugees from Hitler. As might be expected, German art from the first half of this century sells as readily in New York or London as it does in Germany itself. Although no contemporary art has yet been included in Sotheby's Munich sales, there is also an adventurous group of German collectors of contemporary art, a sign that art holds an important place in the country's culture.

Selections from last year's sales were exhibited in Cologne, Vienna, Zurich, Frankfurt and Hamburg, attracting large crowds at every centre. They were finally hung against the elegant pale yellow walls of Munich's newly enlarged and redecorated saleroom. The twentieth-century painting sale was held first, on 28 October 1987. The saleroom was crowded to overflowing, with over 600 people and a barrage of telephones to take bids from overseas clients. In the event, German private collectors carried off four of the five top lots, though the most expensive painting in the sale was bought by an American private collector. This was Max Beckmann's *Bar, Braun,* painted in Amsterdam in 1944 (DM605,000).

There were several works in the sale by Hermann Max Pechstein, a member of the Expressionist Die Brücke group, which also included Ernst Ludwig Kirchner and Erich Heckel. All sold well, with *Rettungsboot* going to a German private collector for DM423,500. A powerful painting of 1911, it shows a moment of high drama with a lifeboat being launched upon a stormy sea. The thick, rhythmic black lines and strong, anti-naturalistic colours show Pechstein at the height of his powers; small wonder that competition for the picture was very strong and it easily doubled its high estimate. Pechstein's *Sonnenflecken,* a calmer scene of boats also displaying his bold colour sense, sold for DM198,000. His *Turm bei Viesole,* 1913, a street scene built up in vivid blocks of pink, blue and yellow, meanwhile

Oskar Kokoschka, Madchen im Blauen Kleid, *watercolour and pencil, 45 by 31 cm, sold 11 November 1987.*

PRICE
DM165,000 (£54,817: $95,376)

comfortably exceeded its top estimate, selling for DM148,500.

The interesting provenance and personal quality of some of the work contributed greatly to the success of the twentieth-century sale. There was a series of postcards with designs in coloured crayons and pen and ink, drawn by Pechstein and his circle and sent to a friend of the group, the photographer Minja Diez-Duehrkoop. They reveal, with wit and childlike directness, little snatches of the artists' lives: a model tying her hair in front of a mirror, by Pechstein; a *Soirée* by Kirchner, also signed by Otto Mueller; a *Cabaret Szene* of demonic gaiety, drawn by Heckel but signed as well by Kirchner (DM38,500). The vitality and informality of the cards captured the imagination of bidders, and the majority exceeded top estimates.

Some of the postcards came from the collection of Dr Ernst Rathenau, who befriended the Expressionists and bought much work directly from

MUNICH

them in the early part of this century; he took his collection with him when he emigrated to America in the 1930s. It included Ludwig Meidner's brutally self-critical *Selbstporträt*, which at DM88,000 made a record for the artist. He also owned a number of very fine drawings, among them Oskar Kokoschka's *Mädchen im Blauen Kleid*, describing with brilliant economy of line and wash the tense yet defiant gait of a child (DM165,000).

It was a sale where the quality of watercolours and drawings easily matched that of the paintings. Otto Dix's spare and bitter *Erinnerung an Le Havre*, depicting a drunken sailor and a prostitute, made a world record for a Dix drawing at DM165,000. It was bought by a German private collector. Another of his countrymen paid DM275,000 for a characteristically soft and glowing watercolour of flowers by Emil Nolde, entitled *Blumenzauber*.

The pattern of high attendance and keen bidding repeated itself at the sale of nineteenth-century German painting on 11 November, with the rooms filled with private collectors and dealers from all over Germany, several Americans present who had flown in especially for the sale, and telephone bids from a number of countries. The substantial group of works by Carl Spitzweg, a mid-nineteenth century 'Biedermeier' painter, proved very popular: perhaps Spitzweg's half-humorous evocations of unchanging small-town life are a comfort in a less settled age. Chief among them was *Die Scharwache*, which went to a private collector for DM748,000, a record for the artist. Painted in Rembrandt-like browns and greys, the theme of the work is the night watch going through the shuttered medieval alleyways of a German town, probably Spitzweg's home city, Munich; moonlight breathes peace on the scene. A dealer from Munich meanwhile paid DM572,000 for Spitzweg's *Sennerin und Mönch*, an amusing scene of a monk distracted from his prayerbook by a glimpse of a young peasant girl's ankle as she climbs a stile. The psychological observation is as deft as the realistic country setting, with the declining sun turning the tips of the grasses to gold.

Other important lots reflected the fascination that Germans have long had with the classical south: for example Leo von Klenze's dignified landscape of 1860, *Ansicht auf der Insel Zante* (DM198,000). Von Klenze, a leading neoclassical architect, stayed in Greece in 1834 with King Otto of Greece, brother of Ludwig I of Bavaria. In addition, nineteenth-century German landscapes cast their spell on modern buyers: Eduard Schleich Snr's mistily romantic *Gebirgslandschaft* was bought on the telephone for DM66,000.

THE US CONSTITUTION

Constitution of the United States, published in The Pennsylvania Packet, and Daily Advertiser, *no. 2690, Philadelphia, Dunlap & Claypoole, Wednesday 19 September 1787, folio 46.4 by 29.1 cm, sold 13 May 1987.*

PRICE
$110,000 (£66,265)

The year 1987 marked the bicentenary of one of the most remarkable documents of American history: the Constitution of the United States, dated 19 September 1787. The Constitution was discussed, written, and ratified at the Constitutional Convention in Philadelphia from 25 May to 17 September 1787, and this is its first authorized publication, in *The Pennsylvania Packet, and Daily Advertiser.* It sold for $110,000, nearly doubling the pre-sale estimate. John Dunlap and David C. Claypoole were the official printers; they also printed two earlier 'draft' editions for the delegates' use.

CAPTAIN UPTON'S HOUSE

The work of Edward Hopper was especially well represented in a sale in New York in December: there were seven paintings and drawings spanning his career from the early 1920s to the mid-1950s. By the mid-1920s, as he approached the age of 40, Hopper had developed a set of compositional approaches and identified a number of themes to which he returned again and again. Two of these, his love of architecture and the sea, were combined in his rendering of *Captain Upton's House*, which sold for a record $2,310,000. Painted in Maine in 1927, this view of the Two Lights at Cape Elizabeth is one of three paintings of the subject, the others being in the Metropolitan Museum of Art, New York, and in Dallas. In each, the stark architectural forms are set against a vivid blue sky and the clear Maine sunlight animates the image.

Edward Hopper, Captain Upton's House, *1927, oil on canvas, 72.5 by 92 cm, sold 3 December 1987.*

PRICE
$2,310,000 (£1,262,295)

A REMARKABLE FIND

This Bugatti was found in a derelict garage outside Hampton Court. The property of the late Kenneth Ullyett J.P., the car was discovered almost by accident.

Kenneth Ullyett, who died ten years ago, was known both as a clock enthusiast and a collector of vintage cars, having written several books on the latter. Following the death of his widow, the executors had called in Sotheby's, in respect of the clocks and furniture remaining in the house. The Bugatti came to the attention of Michael Turner, Sotheby's expert in clocks and watches, who rang Malcolm Barber, Director of Vintage Cars, to enquire how much such a Bugatti might be worth; the reply was 'between £10,000 and £5 million, depending upon year, model and condition', and Mr Barber was soon on the scene.

The Bugatti as it was found in the derelict garage.

Considerable muscle was needed to gain access to the garage, the doors being obstructed by foliage and heavy undergrowth. Behind all this, the building was ramshackle, with its doors hanging off and a collapsed roof, but it was found to be housing not only the Bugatti, but a whole selection of extraordinary motor vehicles. There was a 'Stanhope' electric car, c. 1902, a Steamobile, c. 1901, and various vintage and veteran car parts, as well as several motorcycles. The cellar of the house also proved an Aladdin's Cave. All the items were sold through Sotheby's last November.

It was no easy task to remove them; the geography of the garden had been altered since the cars were first placed there. In the case of the Bugatti, which was in sound condition but requiring total restoration, just one tyre needed to be blown up in order to roll it out. It had probably been in store for twenty years, maybe longer.

Bugatti Type 57 Atlante Coupé, c. 1938, sold 30 November 1987.

PRICE
£79,200 ($136,224)

THE COLLECTION OF
FLORA WHITNEY MILLER

Flora Whitney Miller, a photograph by Baron de Meyer.

Flora Whitney Miller, whose estate came up for sale last spring, was the granddaughter of Cornelius Vanderbilt II and William C. Whitney, and the daughter of Harry Payne Whitney and the vivacious Gertrude Vanderbilt Whitney. She was surrounded from birth by art and furnishings of the highest quality. Her childhood home was a 54-room mansion at 871 Fifth Avenue which had been decorated by the celebrated Stanford White, the most fashionable designer of the period.

The collecting traditions of both the Whitneys and the Vanderbilts were well established by the time of Flora's birth in 1897. Her father, Harry Payne Whitney, was one of the great sportsmen of his day. He passed this passion on to his daughter who later in life had a fierce attachment to the New York Mets, a team that her cousin Joan Whitney Payson owned. He brought his sense of sport into the auction-room as well, bidding often for distraction but also, when challenged, to win.

One such occasion was the Yerkes sale of 1910 at the American Art Association. Whitney had already purchased a pair of paintings by Guardi at a rather modest price, and these were to be followed on the block by a third larger and more stately painting of the Grand Canal. When this came up, Whitney bid in quite small advances of $50. Henry Duveen, one of the doyens among art dealers, was evidently a bit peeved at the millionaire's apparent parsimony and raised the bid by $500. Whitney continued in increments of $50, Duveen in sums of $500, until the bid had reached $17,000, more than ten times the price that Whitney had paid for either of the two other paintings. In a reverse of strategy, Whitney decided to jump the bid to $20,000, easily outdistancing Duveen with one bid. Not a poor winner, but again not above a bit of gloating, he stood up in his place and chided Duveen, exclaiming, 'You made me pay for that' in front of an amused room.

Flora's mother, Gertrude, took art much more seriously. She kept a studio in Paris on the Rue Boileau, and another on the family estate at Old Westbury, Long Island. Her generosity to other artists was as great as it was discreet: John Sloan wrote in 1949 that there were 'innumerable artists whose studio rent was paid, or pictures purchased just at the right time to keep the wolf from the door, or hospital expenses covered, or a trip to Europe made possible'. She was one of a very small group interested in contemporary American art, and her greatest achievement was the foundation and funding in 1930 of the Whitney Museum of American Art, to support these struggling American artists by giving them a showcase and making purchases for a permanent collection. It was to Flora, however, that the museum was later to owe its survival. She guided it for over twenty-five years, helped it to change with the times, and more than once saved it from oblivion.

Her dedication to the Whitney Museum is not only witnessed by the time and energy she devoted to it, but by the donations she made to it. On 14 October 1965 she sold her painting *Le Fumeur* by Edouard Manet for the museum, the hammer price being $450,000. Similarly, she donated her sculpture *Jeune Fille Qui Marche Dans L'Eau; Etude Pour L'Ile De France* by Aristide Maillol to a benefit auction held at Parke-Bernet to raise money for the Whitney's present galleries. The sculpture raised $37,000, the most expensive lot in the sale by a considerable margin. But her greatest gesture was made on 29 May 1980 when *Juliet and Her Nurse* by J.M.W. Turner was sold at Sotheby's. This glowing, misty, magnificent vision of Venice was her favourite painting and when she moved from one to another of her houses, it travelled with her. In her New York apartment it was given a place of honour above her Vanderbilt grandmother's elaborately carved and gilt grand piano. Considered the most important Turner still in a private collection – Martin Butlin, Keeper of the historic British collection at the Tate Gallery, described it as 'perhaps the most splendid of all Turner's paintings of the 1830s' – it had been taken to America by Flora's great-uncle, Colonel O.H. Payne, in 1901. Her affection was certainly not unwarranted: *Juliet and Her Nurse* was sold for $7.04 million, then the highest price paid for a work of art at auction, and a substantial share went to the Whitney Museum.

The sales held in the spring of 1987, after Flora's death, were a monument to the variety of her taste and to the confidence with which she put together and lived with the objects she had collected and inherited. The Steinway Louis XVI-style painted and parcel-gilt grand piano, the one above which the Turner had hung, brought $60,500 – more than three times its top estimate. Two of her fine Beauvais tapestries made more than $22,000 each.

Among the highlights of her collection perhaps the most interesting was the Roman sarcophagus from the studio garden at Old Westbury. This had been brought back from Europe by her mother, probably during her first trip to Athens and Rome with her husband in 1901–2. As a sculptor, Gertrude had had a fascination with the object and had even expressed a desire to create one for herself. After her death, the sarcophagus, although not neglected, was not regarded as well as it might have been. It became a place for the younger members of Flora's family to play in at times, and there is a story that it was once used as a tub for geraniums. Despite all of this, the sarcophagus was recognized as a masterpiece of antique art and made $275,000, then a record

Roman marble sarcophagus, second quarter of the 3rd century AD, 101 by 203.4 by 99 cm, sold 29 May 1987.

PRICE
$275,000 (£165,626)

Mary Cassatt, The Letter *(B.146), c. 1891, drypoint with soft ground and aquatint printed in colours, 35.7 by 22.8 cm (image), 33.4 by 20.3 cm (sheet), sold 13 May 1987.*

PRICE
$192,500 (£115,964)

for a piece of Roman sculpture. It now resides in the Antichen Museen in Berlin, whose collection of Greek and Roman antiquities is considered among the finest in the world.

Two prints by Mary Cassatt entitled *The Letter* and *Feeding the Ducks* demonstrated Flora's own level of connoisseurship, even in a field as difficult as prints. She bought both at the Robert Harthorne Gallery Sale at the Parke-Bernet Galleries in 1946. *The Letter* is a fabulous image, heavily influenced by the Japanese woodblock prints that were beginning to flood into the West at the end of the nineteenth century. Cassatt only made twenty-five impressions, using a special printing technique called 'à la poupée' in which the artist colours the plate by hand. The result is a painterly and unique effect in each print. This print, then, because of its rarity, its direct association with the artist and its good condition, made $192,500. *Feeding the Ducks* is an equally charming scene showing two women and an infant feeding ducks from a rowing-boat. The technique employed here was more straightforward, but the impression was fine and the condition good; it secured a price of $88,000, twice its estimate.

Other items included two pieces of Paul de Lamerie silver. The first, a salver dated 1736, was decorated in an extremely lively manner with cast strapwork, shells, scalework, and monster heads, the centre engraved with flamboyant rococo scrolling and shells and the arms of Maynard. It brought $60,500. The second piece was a beautiful pierced cake basket dated two years later, but lacking none of the robust rococo qualities of the salver. Decorated in a similar manner, the cake basket was inscribed 'Gertrude Vanderbilt from George W. Vanderbilt Aug: 25. 1896' which identified it as a wedding present to Flora's mother from her cousin. Engraved with the coat of arms of the Earl of Hardwicke, it made $66,000.

Undoubtedly the most spectacular lots in the sale were Mrs Miller's jewellery, which ranged from the whimsical to the sublime. There was an unusual diamond and ruby 'Comet' brooch, dating from about 1910, which made $99,000. The head was a 5-carat diamond and the tail was formed of rows of diamonds and rubies set *en tremblant*. This sporty piece of jewellery must have been meant to represent Halley's comet which made its appearance in 1910. Perhaps it reflects the somewhat cavalier attitude of the young Whitneys: the headlines that year had proclaimed doom for the

Diamond and ruby 'Comet' brooch, mounted in platinum and gold, c. 1910, sold 27 April 1987.

PRICE
$99,000 (£61,491)

105

A diamond necklace with a triple-row collar, c. 1915, sold 27 April 1987.

PRICE
$880,000 (£546,584)

An emerald and diamond leaf brooch, signed Cartier 51-31453, sold 27 April 1987.

PRICE
$715,000 (£444,099)

human race when the comet's tail, laden with poisonous gases, swung by the earth. Another brooch, while of a much less exotic form than the 'Comet', far surpassed it in the fabulous quality of its largest gem. An emerald and diamond leaf brooch by Cartier, it featured a 12.31-carat emerald-cut emerald of such exceptional colour and clarity that it has been called one of the finest ever offered at auction. The quality of this stone pushed the brooch up to a price of $715,000, more than twice its estimate. However, the piece of jewellery that most truly reflected the opulence of the Whitneys' world was the magnificent diamond necklace, dating from the last years of the Gilded Age. It is not difficult to imagine Gertrude Whitney wearing this to any of the elaborate fêtes celebrated at Newport or Saratoga. Made *c.* 1915, of more than 230 diamonds weighing together more than 145.73 carats, the necklace was designed as a triple-row collar with a series of large graduated pear-shaped diamonds as pendants. It sold for $880,000.

PUNTS MEETING

*P*unts Meeting fetched a record price for the artist, Stanley Spencer, when it was sold in November 1987: at £429,000 it achieved more than five times the previous record, which had been set in June. Painted in 1953, it was intended to be the first in a cycle of paintings called *Christ Preaching at Cookham Regatta*. The title alone suggests the strange paradox that makes Spencer's work so unique. Christ, accompanied by his disciples, visits the village of Cookham to preach from the horse-ferry barge moored by Cookham Bridge. Drawing on his memories of the annual Cookham Regatta, before the First World War, Spencer used this small Berkshire village to symbolize the earthly paradise. Painted as if from the bridge where the artist and his brother had stood watching the Regatta forty years earlier, the picture recalls the time when, too poor to own a punt, Spencer had felt that to sit in one seemed 'an unattainable Eden'.

Sir Stanley Spencer, RA, Christ Preaching at Cookham Regatta: Punts Meeting, *1953, oil on canvas, 79 by 129.5 cm, sold 11 November 1987.*

PRICE
£429,000 ($810,810)

KAFKA'S LETTERS TO FELICE

On 20 September 1912 Kafka wrote his first letter to Felice Bauer, opening a five-year correspondence that has been described as 'the most precise and exacting history of a human relationship'. In these letters, postcards and telegrams, Kafka reveals himself with startling candour, describing in detail his feelings of alienation and helplessness, his ambivalence about marriage, his aspirations and frustrations, his physical and spiritual illness.

His confidante, Felice Bauer, was a plain, capable, well-intentioned young woman from Berlin, who clearly loved him, but who never began to fathom his genius. For Kafka, her orderly, conventional life in Berlin provided a source of stability and strength that was sufficiently remote not to intrude on his seclusion in Prague. Throughout their affair, which encompassed ruptures and reconciliations and two broken engagements, Kafka struggled with his belief in the strength her presence could give him and his need for solitude. In January 1913 he wrote: 'Writing means revealing oneself to excess ... This is why one can never be alone enough when one writes, why there never can be enough silence around when one writes'.

Yet the period of their relationship is also that of Kafka's greatest literary achievement. In a single night, just a few days after they met, Kafka wrote *The Judgement*, the work with which he felt that he had finally become a writer. Here the central but unseen female figure, Frieda Brandenfeld (Felice Bauer) is the fiancée of the protagonist. Very soon thereafter Kafka wrote *The Metamorphosis*, again influenced by his new affair. Direct connections can also be demonstrated to *Amerika*, the 'Letter to his Father' and above all *The Trial*. In this novel, the arrest and trial of Joseph K. have clear parallels in Kafka's descriptions of his feelings of entrapment by Felice's family at the time of their engagement and his powerlessness at the 'tribunal' that dissolved their contract. In fact, virtually everything Kafka wrote in his twelve remaining years has significant roots in these letters.

Felice Bauer preserved this correspondence for most of her life, ultimately selling the archive to Schocken Books, Inc., which published the letters after her death in 1960 and offered them for sale last summer.

Left. *Franz Kafka with Felice Bauer.*
Below. *A letter from the collection of 327 autograph letters, 15 typed letters, 145 autograph postcards, 33 typed postcards, and 5 telegrams which constituted Franz Kafka's correspondence with Felice Bauer, 20 September 1912 to 16 October 1917, sold 18 June 1987.*

PRICE
$605,000 (£371,166)

THE CHESTERFIELD WINE COOLERS

These two wine coolers formed part of the service of plate issued to Philip Dormer Stanhope, 4th Earl of Chesterfield, on his appointment as Ambassador to the Netherlands in 1727. They were originally ice pails, being converted to wine coolers at the beginning of the nineteenth century. Following the custom on such an appointment, the Jewel Office was issued with a warrant, dated 12 September 1727, to supply Chesterfield with 'the usual allowance' of plate; 5,893 oz. of white and 1,066 oz. of gilt. Tracked down in the records, these 'ice pailes' originally cost £252 13s. 9d.

Chesterfield is remembered best for his copious letter-writing. 'A Wit among Lords and a Lord among Wits', according to Dr Johnson, he was less generously described by George II on one occasion as 'a little gossiping tea table scoundrel'. He began a distinguished political career as a Member of Parliament, becoming an active member of the House of Lords on his father's death in 1726 – although he had hitherto dismissed the place as 'a hospital for incurables'.

Within months of George II's accession in 1727, he was nominated Lord of the Bedchamber and a Privy Councillor. At the King's behest, Walpole offered Chesterfield the English Embassy at The Hague shortly afterwards, a post which he eagerly accepted.

Above. *Philip Dormer Stanhope, 4th Earl of Chesterfield (1694-1773).*

Opposite. *One of a pair of George II ambassadorial wine-coolers, maker's mark of Paul Crespin struck over that of Paul de Lamerie, London, 1727, height 26.5 cm, sold 4 February 1988.*

PRICE
£462,000 ($859,320)

The auction in progress.

VAN GOGH'S IRISES

*I*rises, one of Vincent Van Gogh's most famous and appealing images, was sold in New York on 11 November 1987 for $53,900,000, the highest price yet paid for a work of art at auction. Ever since it was painted in May 1889, the picture has been recognized as one of Van Gogh's masterpieces. Submitted to the Salon des Indépendants that year, it was praised by the artist's brother Theo as 'a beautiful study, full of air and life'.

Irises was painted soon after Van Gogh's admission to the asylum of Saint Paul de Mausole in St Rémy, Provence. He entered the hospital as a voluntary patient on 8 May 1889 after several difficult months in Arles, following his rupture with Gauguin. His physician, Dr Peyron, recorded that he was

> suffering from acute mania with hallucinations of sight and hearing which have caused him to mutilate himself by cutting off his right ear. At present he seems to have recovered his reason, but he does not feel that he possesses the strength and courage to live independently and has voluntarily asked to be admitted to this institution.

Van Gogh began to paint within a few days, taking his subjects from the pleasantly untended asylum garden.

Floral themes were always important subjects for him and the iris was particularly significant because of its importance in Japanese art, which he especially admired. Provence with its strong light and clear skies provided a European equivalent to his idealized vision of Japan, and its abundant vegetation was a source of infinite inspiration. Van Gogh had first painted

David J. Nash, Director of the Impressionist Painting Department, receives the winning bid by telephone.

the iris during his stay in Arles and this majestic flower was to be the subject of three further paintings, a second view of irises growing painted later the same month in St Rémy, and two views of the flowers cut and arranged in vases, which are among his last works painted at the asylum.

The greatest of these, however, is *Irises*. The painful contrast between this exuberant vision of nature and its creator's tortured mental state has a perpetual fascination. Claude Monet expressed this tension most succinctly: 'How did a man who loved flowers and light to such an extent and who rendered them so well, how then did he still manage to be so unhappy?'

First owned by Père Tanguy, *Irises* passed through a number of distinguished collections before it was acquired by Joan Whitney Payson for $87,000 in 1947. The daughter of Payne Whitney and Helen Hay Whitney, Mrs Payson was born into a family whose cultural and philanthropic interests are legendary in the United States. She and her brother Jock grew up in a Fifth Avenue mansion designed by the fashionable turn-of-the-century architect Stanford White, surrounded by a collection of paintings assembled by their father that ranged from Rembrandt to Sargent. After his death in 1927, they shared his estate of $179 million, then one of the largest fortunes in America. From their mother, they inherited the famous Greentree Racing Stables. Helen Hay Whitney was also the source of Mrs Payson's passion for baseball, which found its fullest expression in her commitment, as an owner

Vincent Van Gogh, Irises, *1889, oil on canvas, 71 by 93 cm, sold 11 November 1987.*

PRICE
$53,900,000 (£29,453,552)

*John Whitney Payson
beaming after the sale of
his mother's painting.*

as well as a fan, to the New York Mets, who rose from obscurity to become World Series champions first in 1969 and most recently in 1986.

Joan Whitney Payson, and her husband, Charles Shipman Payson, an eminently successful businessman, continued the Whitney tradition in the arts, forming a collection that has been described by François Daulte, their friend and advisor and a prominent authority on Impressionism, as one of the finest in the United States. *Irises* became its centrepiece and Mrs Payson's favourite. For many years the painting hung over the mantelpiece in the drawing-room of their New York apartment, complemented by works by Gauguin and Rousseau but clearly dominating the room.

When Mrs Payson died in 1975, her son John Whitney Payson inherited *Irises* and he consigned it for sale last autumn. By the time the painting appeared in the saleroom, it had completed a 17,000-mile tour of Sotheby's international offices in Europe and the Far East, returning for exhibition in New York. More than 2,000 people filled the room for the sale itself, and the crowd gasped as John L. Marion, chairman of Sotheby's in North America, opened the bidding at $15 million and proceeded in increments of $1 million. After a heated duel between two telephone bidders, the winning bid was made by a European representing an anonymous collector.

After the sale, a beaming John Payson accepted an iris for his lapel and announced that he was ecstatic about the result and that both his mother and Van Gogh would have been stunned by the price. A portion of the proceeds was donated to a group of cultural organizations in Maine, Charles S. Payson's native state.

LINCOLN'S LETTER TO 'THE OTHER MARY'

Abraham Lincoln, America's sixteenth president, remains the most popular in the market for presidential manuscripts. This letter documents his only romantic attachment before the courtship of Mary Todd, whom he married in 1842. Mary Owens, known as the 'other Mary', was visiting her sister in Illinois when she met Lincoln in 1833. Three years later Lincoln promised Mary's sister that he would propose, but after this separation, he found Mary Owens less attractive than he had remembered. In this letter to her dated 7 May 1837, it is clear that Lincoln had second thoughts about their informal engagement. He leaves the decision to Mary, but writes, 'my opinion is that you had better not do it'. Later, in a note to his sister, Lincoln gave a wryly humorous account of how he 'got out of it' and how Mary Owens declined his proposal. Lincoln's note to the 'other Mary' brought $77,000, a record for a letter by Lincoln.

Above. *Mary Owens*

Left. *Abraham Lincoln, sixteenth president of the USA, autograph letter to Mary Owens, signed Lincoln, 7 May 1837, 1½ pages small folio, sold 23 October 1987.*

PRICE
$77,000 (£46,386)

115

THE BÉHAGUE COLLECTION

An Ostrogothic gold and garnet eagle brooch, 5th century AD, from the Domagnano Treasure, height 12 cm, sold 5 December 1987.

PRICE
FF14,400,000 (£1,414,538: $2,588,605)

Although Monaco has become a major international auction centre in recent years, it was nevertheless an unusual location for the sale of the great collection of antiquities and works of art formed during the early years of this century by the almost legendary French collector and patron of the arts, Martine, Comtesse de Béhague (1870–1939). But it was here, amidst the stuccoed splendour of the Principality, almost within sight of her friend Théodore Reinach's eccentric Grecian-style Villa Kerylos at Beaulieu-sur-Mer and only a couple of hours' drive from her own somewhat more conventional villa at Hyères, that the Comtesse's collection was dispersed by Sotheby's on 5 December 1987.

A collection of this type, comprising material drawn principally from the ancient civilizations of the Mediterranean, but with a sprinkling of later objects ranging in date from the Dark Ages to the Renaissance, would normally have been sold in London, which is still the pre-eminent European centre for important sales of antiquities and early works of art. However, in accordance with the wishes of the vendors, who were the great nephews of the Comtesse herself, the Marquis de Ganay and his brothers, the decision was taken to hold the sale in Monaco, which is the closest selling centre to metropolitan France and the newly buoyant French market to which Sotheby's has access. The prices that were achieved, many of them world records in their respective categories, fully vindicated that decision but, in the summer of 1987, when work on preparing the sale began, the prospect was fraught with uncertainties. Never before had any auction house offered objects of such a highly specialized nature in Monaco.

Building on the worldwide fame and renown of the collection, the decision was taken to present the sale as an art-market event with an international dimension. A travelling exhibition was organized, comprising all but a few of the most important objects, and this went on view in New York, London and Stuttgart. For most of the prospective buyers, it was to be their first opportunity to see at close hand a group of antiquities and works of art which before had been known to them only by way of articles and faded photographs in scholarly publications. The exhibition provoked enormous interest and there were to be many surprises and discoveries in store for those who came to view. One distinguished museum curator, whose acquaintance with the collection had been confined to the learned literature, inquired why it was that Sotheby's was exhibiting items from the collection of the Comtesse de Béarn alongside those from the collection of the Comtesse de Béhague, only to learn that the two were one and the same, the Comtesse having reverted to her maiden name following her divorce from Comte René de Béarn. It was during the period of the Comtesse's marriage, however, that a catalogue of her collection was published by one of the curators at the Louvre, Wilhelm Froehner, with the result that it became known to subsequent generations as the collection of the Comtesse de Béarn.

By 1987, Froehner's catalogue, despite the excellence of its scholarship, was out of date in many respects. Not only did the Comtesse continue adding to her collection long after its publication, but many of Froehner's original attributions had undergone considerable revision in the years that followed. The virtual inaccessibility of the collection meant that this process of reassessment was largely unsystematic, springing solely from the particular interests of scholars working in widely disparate fields. References to some of the major items in the collection were scattered across a wide range of publications, so that, when Sotheby's own experts came to grapple with the task of preparing the auction catalogue, they found themselves ferreting through a polyglot mountain of antiquarian literature in search of odd scraps of information. To compound these difficulties, it was soon discovered that many of the Comtesse's own records had been either mislaid or destroyed, with the result that much of the background detail that is essential to the production of a scholarly auction catalogue was totally lacking. Never again, however, would there be an opportunity to see this part of the Béhague Collection assembled together and the resulting catalogue, with its 296 lots, was intended not just as a guide for prospective buyers but as an essential work of reference. Seen from another point of view, it was also a tribute to the memory of the Comtesse and it was certainly in this spirit that the Marquis de Ganay himself wrote a short but elegant introduction, in which he evoked his childhood recollections of his great-aunt and briefly summarized the recent history of the collection.

The auction was an outstanding success, the sale of antiquities setting a new record in this field – over FF48,000,000 – as buyers from all over the world competed furiously to secure their chosen lots. The famous Ostrogothic gold and garnet eagle brooch from the Domagnano Treasure sold to a New York buyer for FF14,400,000, itself a world record for a single antiquity at auction; a small Egyptian ivory figure of a young nude woman, just over four inches high, sold for FF3,100,000; and another, but this time in wood and measuring seven inches in height, sold for FF3,900,000. The Béhague Apollo, a celebrated Greek bronze of the fifth century BC, sold to a private European collector for FF8,300,000. Although the second session, in which works of art were auctioned, contained fewer acknowledged masterpieces, the prices fetched were scarcely less high in certain instances, with two very rare examples of Saint-Porchaire faience of the sixteenth century fetching FF4,100,000 and FF2,800,000 respectively. The latter was among the objects from the collection bought by the Réunion des Musées Nationaux on behalf of the national museums of France, there to join three other wonderful pieces that had previously been donated by the Marquis de Ganay and his brothers as a fitting tribute to the memory of their great-aunt, the Comtesse de Béhague.

A Greek bronze figure of Apollo, second quarter of the 5th century BC, height 12 cm, sold 5 December 1987.

PRICE
FF8,300,000 (£815,324: $1,492,043)

LA PETITE DANSEUSE DE QUATORZE ANS

When the wax original of this cast of Degas's *Petite Danseuse de Quatorze Ans* was exhibited at the sixth Impressionist exhibition in 1881, the public was profoundly shocked. The unconventional pose and the fatigue evident in the figure contrasted sharply with the idealized forms of the marble sculpture to which the nineteenth-century audience was accustomed. One critic wrote, 'The bourgeois admitted to contemplate this wax creature remain stupefied for a moment and one hears the father's cry "God forbid my daughter should become a dancer".'

The most ambitious of Degas's surviving sculptures, the *Petite Danseuse de Quatorze Ans* is also the only one for which there are numerous studies. In addition to the works on paper, Degas executed a preparatory nude study of the figure, roughly three-quarters of the size of the exhibited work.

The model for this very thorough survey was Marie van Goethem. The daughters of a Belgian laundress and tailor, Marie and her sisters Antoinette and Louise-Josephine were ballet students at the Opéra. These young girls, the 'rats' of the Opéra, the raw material from which the 'stars' were formed, were of particular interest to Degas at this time and his poignant Mante Family portrait of *c.* 1884 shows two of them under the supervision of their attentive mother.

Petite Danseuse was the only one of Degas's sculptures exhibited in his lifetime and none was cast until after his death. This bronze is one of a limited number of casts made by the Hébrard Foundry in the 1920s and was retained by the Hébrard family for several years. It was acquired by the well-known American collectors Jack and Belle Linsky at Sotheby's in New York for $380,000 in 1971 and resold on behalf of Mrs Linsky's Estate on 10 May of this year for $10,120,000, a record for sculpture at auction.

THE ROMANOV PHOTOGRAPH ALBUMS

Three previously unknown photograph albums assembled by members of the Russian Imperial Family – the Consort and children of Emperor Alexander III – recently passed through Sotheby's saleroom.

The owners and compilers of the albums were all keen photographers and many of these images show them to have been very professional. In some pictures it is possible even to catch a glimpse of the cameras they used. There are several such shots of Dowager Empress Maria Feodorovna, widow of Alexander III and mother of the late Tsar, Nicholas II. There is also one of her youngest son, Grand Duke Michael, photographed in the act of taking his own portrait reflected in a mirror, with the use of a tripod!. Another character with a camera is the strikingly handsome Grand Duke Dimitri Pavlovich, a favourite of the family, who later (1916) became implicated in the gruesome assassination of Grigory Rasputin.

Photography was taken seriously; someone was always on hand to develop the film, and the photographs were brought for inspection in the evening. Selecting them and glueing them in place was a favourite pastime and

Below. A sequence showing Michael and (below) Olga swinging on a trapeze in an improvised gym. Olga wrote the caption 'Acrobats' beside the pictures in her album.

Below right. Olga and Michael with their pet dogs Lipka and Blek.

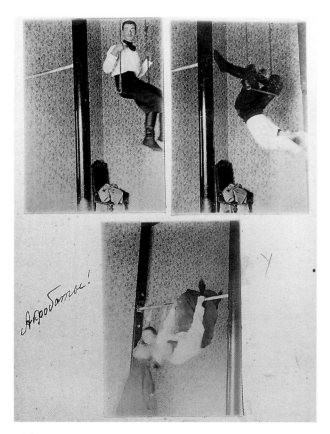

scrapbooks lay in profusion throughout the private apartments in the Imperial residences. There is even a shot of the Dowager Empress and her younger daughter, the Grand Duchess Olga, leafing through an album – perhaps the very one sold. The photographs are fascinating for what they show of intimate domestic life in the splendid eighteenth-century palaces, where they lived so informally: Gatchina, with its twin towers and low vaulted ceilings, set in a secluded park with extensive stables and kennels for hunting, its rivers and lakes teeming with fish; the small and intimate Alexandria Pavilion on the Gulf of Finland at Peterhov; and the official residence of the Dowager Empress in St Petersburg, the Anichkov. The photographs show many private mementoes surrounding the sitters. There are paintings by Aivazovsky (a favourite artist of Alexander III) and family photographs in great profusion. The Dowager Empress poses in the drawing-room with its fitted floral carpets and comfortable chairs. One shot – taken in the Anichkov – of a desk and above it a mirror with photographs stuck casually under the frame is inscribed in Grand Duchess Olga's hand 'my room'. Her brother Michael appears in his album drinking tea from a samovar beneath a massive stuffed bison, with his portrait by Repin in the background – this was a study for the artist's monumental painting of Russia's Upper House, the Council of the Empire.

The earliest album in the sale belonged to Grand Duchess Olga (1882–1960), and is dated Peterhof 1896. Generous, and with disarmingly simple tastes, Olga liked to surround herself with ordinary people and especially representatives of the Russian peasant class, with whom she had a strong affinity. She was good at sport and a talented watercolourist. Her albums show pet dogs: 'Lipka' and her brother Michael's dog 'Black'

A group including Grand Duchess Yelena Vladimirovna (mother of Princess Marina of Kent) and Olga with her arm around her English nanny Miss Franklin.

121

Emperor Nicholas II blesses the troops of the 37th Infantry Division, while his mother, in the foreground, looks on.

(transliterated from the English into the nearest Russian equivalent as 'Blek'). There are family groups, including a youthful, still beardless Nicholas II shown with his brother and English Royal cousins before his accession.

Olga often appears in a playful mood; she is remembered as something of a tomboy. Photographs show her somersaulting in the grass, running, jumping, rowing, doing the can-can and tobogganing. In one sequence of shots with Michael, she appears dangling from ropes and a trapeze in an improvised gym against a background of floral wallpaper. Underneath she has written in her own hand 'acrobats', and in the adjoining shot which shows her and Misha grinning at the camera, 'resting'. Nicholas also found time to exercise in the gym next to his study in the Winter Palace. Exercising, he said, helped to clear his head; without it he couldn't think straight.

Under spreading branches by a lake, there appears the unmistakable back view of the old Empress, while next to her her daughters Olga and Xenia and Xenia's sailor husband turn to face the camera, in an atmospheric shot where the play of light is reminiscent of Impressionism. Another group shows the Grand Duchess Yelena Vladimirovna, subsequently Princess Nicholas of Greece and mother of Princess Marina of Kent, and Olga standing with her arm around the shoulders of an old retainer. This is Miss Franklin, the English governess. There is no doubt that the Dowager Empress resented the influence of 'that odious woman' over her wilful daughter. Even when Olga was grown up she refused to contemplate Miss Franklin's replacement by a lady-in-waiting, declaring that she would rather run off with the Palace sweep to work as a kennel maid. Needless to say, the nanny stayed.

Another curious character – also English – flits through these pages. He is the jovial Charles Heath, tutor to the Imperial children. His unobtrusive yet formative influence on Nicholas II has not, perhaps, been sufficiently recognized. Was it from Heath that Nicholas learned to conceal his emotions to an excessive degree, even for someone of his exalted station? In the throes of a crisis volatile Russians were astonished when he talked blandly about the 'beastly weather we're having'! Another English connection, recorded by Olga's camera, was the journey on the two Imperial yachts (belonging to her brother the Emperor and to her mother) to Reval, on the Gulf of Finland, in 1908. The object of this expedition was to meet Edward VII and his consort, a sister of the Dowager Empress, who had come to cement the Anglo-Russian *entente*. The photographs include one of an English admiral arm in arm with the old Empress.

The album of Olga's elder sister Xenia (1875–1960) relates to the period of 1904, the year of the disastrous war with Japan. On 16 July Xenia was present and recorded a parade where her brother Nicholas II reviewed the troops of the 37th Infantry Division prior to their departure for the Far East: officers kissing the hand of the Dowager Empress – a diminutive figure imbued nonetheless with an imposing presence; troops kneeling to receive the blessing of the Orthodox Tsar, who holds aloft an icon of the Saviour; and many others.

Another revealing series of albums, put together by Grand Duke Michael, covers the period 1899–1911. Michael was close to Olga in temperament and they had been brought up together. His great defects were said to be an excessive good nature and his credulity. Although he had no interest in public life, Michael twice found himself in the public eye. The first was occasioned by his controversial liaison with a twice-divorced woman of strong character, a sort of Russian Mrs Simpson. The photographs chronicle and celebrate their love for one another. They also show Michael's fondness for simple country pursuits: there are dogs and a pet bear. House parties arranged for hunting include the composer Rachmaninov among the intimate circle – in one photograph he appears on skis.

The abdication crisis of 1917 propelled Michael into the limelight again, for when Nicholas II renounced the throne both for himself and the sick Tsarevich, the succession passed to his brother. This was an onerous responsibility beyond Michael's natural gifts and he, too, abdicated. Nicholas was appalled by what he regarded as a supreme dereliction of duty. Both Xenia and Olga declined to marry foreign princes because they wanted to go on living in their native land. Both, however, were destined to live a life of exile, dying in the same year (1960), Xenia in a grace and favour home at Hampton Court and Olga in a modest flat above a shop in Toronto. Grand Duke Michael perished in 1918 in the Siberian capital of Perm where he was shot, along with his English secretary, in circumstances that have never been satisfactorily explained.

Xenia's album, sold in February 1986, fetched £30,800. Fifteen months later, in May 1987, Michael's three albums sold for a total of £30,800, and the three assembled by Olga, sold in the same auction, realized £37,400.

Grand Duke Michael Alexandrovich with his mistress.

SPORTING PAINTINGS

George Stubbs, ARA,
Baron de Robeck Riding a
Bay Cob, *1791, oil on
canvas, 101.5 by 127 cm,
sold 4 June 1987.*

PRICE
$2,420,000 (£1,457,831)

Two recent sales confirm the continuing popularity of sporting paintings with American collectors. At $2,420,000 George Stubbs's portrait of the 2nd Baron de Robeck proved not only a record for this artist, but also the highest price ever paid at auction for a sporting painting. The equestrian portrait was one of Stubbs's specialities. This example shows de Robeck, a Swedish nobleman who fought in the American War of Independence and ultimately settled in Ireland, as a country gentleman at ease in a country landscape. The portrait had been sold at Sotheby's London in 1972 for £130,000, then a large sum. The eleven-fold increase is an indication of the strength of this market and it was bought by an American collector. Returning to Sotheby's salerooms after seven years, Sir Alfred Munnings's *Start at Newmarket* established a new world record

for the artist in New York at $1,210,000. On its previous appearance in London in June 1980, it had also made a record at £138,600 ($325,710). Munnings was a passionate racegoer, who had seen 'quite a thousand starts on Newmarket Heath' and never tired of them. He painted several pictures on this theme, of which this is the largest and most effective. Not surprisingly, Munnings was an admirer of Stubbs, exclaiming over another work 'What a good picture, what design, and what a sky.' The artist has been a firm favourite with American collectors for more than a decade; *Start at Newmarket* was part of an American private collection of sporting paintings and it found another US buyer.

Sir Alfred Munnings, PRA, Start at Newmarket: Study No. 4, *oil on board, 92 by 183 cm, sold 29 October 1987.*

PRICE
$1,210,000 (£742,331)

THE GLORIOUS REVOLUTION OF 1688

The year 1988 marks the tercentenary of the Glorious Revolution, when William of Orange and his wife Mary, the elder daughter of James II of England, were secretly invited to take over the English throne. In the event, the Revolution was a comparatively bloodless affair, achieved with Parliament's consent, but it was a historical milestone. The threat of absolute monarchy was lifted and the nature of the Revolution marked the growing power of Parliament. Sales at Sotheby's in 1988 contained a number of important works of art associated with the reign of William and Mary.

In March a private sale to the Rijksmuseum in Amsterdam was arranged for a ring given by Queen Mary to General Godart van Ginkel, a career soldier, for his support during the Irish campaigns that followed the transfer of power. These attempted to stabilize the kingdom by subjugating the outlying Catholic regions where James still had support. To Ginkel fell the difficult task of capturing the key fortress of western Ireland, Athlone, which was so well defended that the enemy commander, St Ruth, said of him: 'His master ought to hang him for trying to take Athlone, and mine ought to hang me if I lose it.' He did lose it and the Queen wrote to Ginkel on 30 June 1691: 'Je vous assure que je n'oublierai jamais ce que vous avez faite' (I promise you that I shall never forget what you have done'). The titles Baron Aughrim, Earl of Athlone, and this ring, are proof that she kept her word.

Another reminder of the turbulent history of Ireland in that period emerged for the Works of Art sale on 21 April; an imposing, if battered, head of William III. Made of lead, it is from the equestrian statue originally

A ring inscribed 'Gift of Queen Mary to General Ginkle [sic] 1st Earl of Athlone 1691', and a gold, enamel and diamond snake bangle, 1856, set with the original rose diamond from Lord Athlone's ring.

The side view of a lead head of William III, Prince of Orange, modelled by John Smyth after Nost the Younger, for the Grinling Gibbons equestrian statue on College Green, Dublin, c. 1836, height 30 cm.

modelled by Grinling Gibbons and erected on College Green, Dublin in 1701. The statue was the butt of abuse from the beginning and William Cobbett remarked that there would never be peace in Dublin until it had been demolished. Damaged parts, including the head, were restored by the Irish sculptor John Smyth in 1836, who followed an earlier bust for the likeness.

The statue, finally destroyed in 1929, makes an appearance in *The Dead*, the last story in James Joyce's great survey of life in the Irish capital, *The Dubliners*, published in 1914. Deciding to drive out to a military review in the park, the Misses Morkan's father harnesses up the mill pony Johnny from the family starch factory. All goes well until they arrive at King Billy's statue, where Johnny takes control: 'and whether he fell in love with the horse King Billy sits on or whether he thought he was back again in the mill, anyhow he began to walk round the statue … Round and round he went'.

THE WRECK OF THE
SS MEDINA

*Lord Carmichael in 1915,
wearing his GCIE and the
KCMG that was recovered
from the wreck of the*
Medina.

O ver the past few years there have been several auction sales of
items recovered from shipwrecks. These wrecks have been very
varied in period and content and in each case have generated much
publicity. Not only the contents themselves but also the hard and
dangerous work that goes into recovering them make a fascinating story.

On 26 May 1988 Sotheby's Billingshurst sold eighty cases of possessions
belonging to Lord Carmichael, Governor of Bengal, lost when the *SS Medina*
was torpedoed by a German U-boat off Devon on 28 April 1917. Lord
Carmichael came from an ancient landowning family in southern Scotland,
following family tradition by devoting his life to public service. He was
Private Secretary to the Secretary of State for Scotland in 1886 and in 1895
won Gladstone's old Liberal seat of Midlothian. From 1908–11 he was
Governor of Victoria, Australia and in 1911 went to India as Governor of
Madras, taking over the Governorship of the newly-constituted Province of
Bengal from 1912 to 1917.

Sir Thomas (later Lord) Carmichael was also a remarkable art collector.
He had gone to Italy in 1885 as a young man with George Curzon (the future
Viceroy of India). From then on he collected works of art voraciously, with
the eclecticism that characterized many late-nineteenth century connoisseurs.
Carmichael's interests ranged from early Renaissance painting and medieval
works of art to rare books and antiquities and, during his time in India, Asian
art. Financial difficulties – chiefly a failure of Hailes Quarry, a major source
of his income – occasioned sales of art and books in 1902 and 1903. As his
finances recovered, Lord Carmichael amassed more objects. These sales, and
the posthumous sale at Sotheby's on 8–10 May 1926, are the only clear
indication of what he owned, as he never made a complete list of his
collection.

Lord Carmichael's time in India was spent in a mixture of administrative
duties, punishing official tours and leisure pursuits, such as balls and hunting
expeditions. The *Medina* baggage reflected these off-duty hours; there were,
for example, tiger skulls from days in the jungles of Cooch Behar. Lord
Carmichael was a keen entomologist whose enthusiasm was rewarded in
India, when he discovered a monstrous new species of daddy-long-legs,
named *Tipula Carmichaeli* after him. His possessions found on board the
Medina included a number of Indian brass figures of insects, among them a
detailed (life size!) six-inch long figure of a centipede.

Despite the distractions available when off duty, Lord Carmichael faced
complex political problems in India. The restructuring of India was one of the
aims of the 1911 Delhi Durbar, a huge traditional gathering at which the
Indian princes paid homage to their King-Emperor George V and Queen
Mary. The royal couple sailed to India in the *Medina*, P&O's most up-to-date
steamship, built at Greenock in 1911 for the mail run to Australia. She was
specially fitted out as a royal yacht, painted in red, white and blue instead of
the usual black and buff livery. Lady Carmichael described the Durbar vividly

in a letter home: the plain full of tents; the gold canopy for the King and Queen; vast processions; bejewelled Indian rulers.

At the Durbar George V announced that the capital of India would be moved from Calcutta (in Bengal, north-east India), to Delhi in the north. Sir Thomas Carmichael was made Governor of the reorganized Province of Bengal, the first since Warren Hastings in 1771, and raised to the peerage as Baron Carmichael. His Indian service brought him three orders of chivalry: Knight Commander of the Order of St Michael and St George; Knight Grand Commander of the Order of the Indian Empire and Knight Grand Commander of the Order of the Star of India. He is wearing his KCMG and GCIE in the photograph of 1915 shown opposite. Both orders went down with the *Medina*; only the KCMG was recovered. It made £154 in the sale, with three masonic items.

With such a broad knowledge of Western art, inevitably Lord Carmichael became fascinated by the art of Asia; an exhibition of Indian, Tibetan, Sikkimese and other artefacts collected by him was held at the Indian Museum, Calcutta in 1915. A large quantity of early twentieth-century Indian brassware was found in Lord Carmichael's *Medina* baggage. The objects were typical crafts of the period, redolent of the vivid and diverse life of colonial India. The sale included religious figures; a group of naturalistic animal studies – among them, most unusually, kangaroos; functional items like candlesticks, plant containers and photo frames, all lavishly ornamented. There were also representations of everyday life, such as three ox-carts transporting captured tigers.

In Spring 1917 the Carmichaels prepared to leave India as the new Governor, Lord MacDonald, arrived to take up his duties. They sailed on the *SS Medina* which, unlike many commercial vessels, had not been commandeered by the Admiralty and was still doing the mail run to Australia. When the Carmichaels embarked at Bombay she was carrying a valuable cargo of tin and Australian meat, much needed in blockaded Britain. The Carmichaels left the *Medina* at Port Said and transferred to the cruiser *Sheffield*, which was faster and better protected against the German navy. Even so, they ran into danger on three occasions before disembarking at Taranto in Italy and continuing their journey overland. They arrived safely in London at the end of April.

The *Medina*, with the Carmichaels' baggage on board, reached Plymouth safely and had started out for Tilbury when she was torpedoed in the late afternoon of 28 April 1917 four miles from Start Point, Devon. Five crew members were killed by the explosion; the rest took to lifeboats in the fortunately calm waters as the *Medina* sank, taking half a decade of Lord Carmichael's life with her. Lord Carmichael returned to a busy life in Britain – visiting his new house at Skirling, taking up City directorships, becoming active in the Burlington Fine Arts Club, museums and masonic affairs – yet his wife said that he felt the loss of his treasured Indian possessions 'to the end of his days'.

The *Medina*'s cargo of tin was salvaged in 1932, but it was not until 1984 that Consortium Recovery Ltd, armed with the most up-to-date diving equipment, decided to try and locate Lord Carmichael's baggage. Although no insurance papers survived, it was felt that, given his fame as a collector, there would be a large number of works of art on the *Medina*. Detailed plans of the ship had been destroyed during the Second World War, but by interviewing survivors of the *Medina*'s last voyage and working from the plans of a sister ship, the likely location of the Carmichael's baggage was estimated.

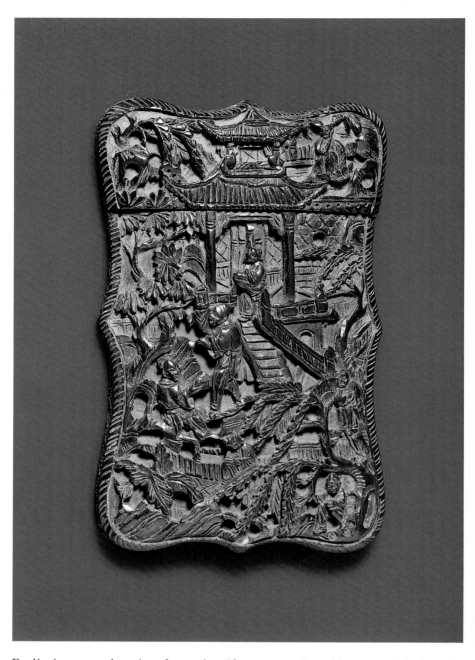

A Chinese ivory card case, second half of the 19th century.

PRICE
£44 ($81)

Preliminary exploration from the *Shearwater Sapphire* revealed that the wreck had been distorted by previous salvage operations; work was later abandoned because of severe weather.

In late 1986 the project was resurrected; Consortium's divers worked this time from the *Holger Dane*, owned by Henning Faddersbøll. The vessel's sophisticated computer position reference systems ensured that the *Holger Dane* remained directly above the wreck without need of an anchor. Work was carried out twenty-four hours a day because of the great expense of the operation. Pairs of divers worked eight-hour shifts from a diving bell lowered 220ft to the wreck. While off duty they remained in pressurized chambers within the ship to avoid time-wasting daily decompression.

Although protected from the intense cold by specially heated suits, the divers faced the hazard of unstable decks and compartments filled with thick mud. Several times they cut through the steel only to find cases of rotting butter and meat. It was decided to abandon the project, until on a final descent one of the divers came on a box marked 'GCIE' (Knight Grand Commander of the Indian Empire) – proof that they had at last found Lord Carmichael's belongings.

There was, as indicated, a large Oriental art collection: Indian brassware, an elaborate wooden chair, a group of earthenware models of fruit; a Japanese tea service; Tibetan temple dogs; a nineteenth-century Chinese ivory card case, elaborately carved with a garden scene. The mud had left many objects in an extraordinarily good state of preservation; all items were stabilized by Consortium's conservation team. There were readable letters from Lord Kitchener and Lord Rosebery; watercolours; even an old Sotheby's coin catalogue. A boot, jars of scent, perfectly-sharpened pencils were brought to the surface. An Assyrian cuneiform seal and bright Ancient Egyptian beads, striped in gold, emerged from the deep. So did Lord and Lady Carmichael's jewels. The latter had historical interest as well as great charm, and attracted keen bidding. A pair of amethyst and diamond sleeve links fetched £1,980 and a collection of Australian black opals £2,145. Opals were first discovered in Queensland in 1872, and were still new to the market in the first decade of this century, when Lord Carmichael was Governor of Victoria. The prices were in response to the high quality of the stones.

Other finds, such as the collection of cups with the P&O cypher reflected life on the steamship; fragments of billiard chalk and a shooting stick told of a leisurely existence long gone. Lord Carmichael's niece recalled the solitary luxury of the Governor's apartments on the *Medina*, as his party sailed away from the last splendours of the Empire into war-ravaged Europe. Lord Carmichael's *Medina* baggage evoked much of the personality of the man, and much of the period. While the sale was not a great one in terms of money realized, the collection in all its variety worked a spell on modern buyers: even the divers were there, bidding for a souvenir.

Jewels belonging to Lord and Lady Carmichael, including, top left, *amethyst and diamond sleeve links;* top right *an amethyst dress suite; and a collection of black opals.*

PRICE
links £1,980 ($3,643); suite £880 ($1,619); opals £2,145 ($3,947)

THE JOHN PAUL JONES 'FREEDOM' BOX

The enamelled medallion that decorates this silver box depicts the famous battle between the *Bon Homme Richard* commanded by John Paul Jones and the *Serapis* under the leadership of Richard Pearson. It is possibly the only known contemporary representation of an event in the American War of Independence. In September 1779, John Paul Jones engaged battle with two British warships off the coast of England. At first, victory for the British seemed assured and Commander Pearson called for an American surrender, whereupon Jones uttered his famous cry, 'I have not yet begun to fight!' The battle turned in favour of the Americans and it was Pearson who ultimately had to surrender. However, in the course of the battle, the commercial fleet, which was sailing under Pearson's protection, was able to escape to safety. This was viewed by the British as a victory and Captain Pearson was honoured by the presentation of this 'freedom' box.

Silver Freedom Box, John Paul Jones, c. 1799, lid with central enamelled medallion, length 10.4 cm, height 5.4 cm, sold 29 January 1988.

PRICE
$66,000 (£35,106)

PHOTOGRAPHS OF THE AMERICAN WEST

Recently discovered in the attic of a country house in the Scottish Highlands, this double-sided English oak screen dates from the 1880s. Carleton Watkins, a pre-eminent photographer of the American West, is known primarily for his photographs of Yosemite Valley, California, and this screen includes many of his most famous images, taken in the 1860s and 1870s. Watkins's large and impressive landscapes of this beautiful valley helped persuade the US Congress to designate the area as a national park and in 1864 President Lincoln signed the Yosemite Bill into law. The screen may have been fashioned for a Scottish traveller who sought to display souvenirs of his 'Grand Tour' of America.

A four-fold double-sided screen composed of 28 photographs of 19th-century America, of which 26 mammoth-plate albumen prints are by Carleton Watkins, 205.7 by 246.4 cm, sold 2 November 1987.

PRICE
$30,250 (£17,587)

DUTCH OLD MASTERS

Above. *Jan Davidsz. de Heem,* Elaborate Still Life on a Cloth-draped Table, *1649, oil on canvas, 75 by 111.5 cm, sold 14 January 1988.*

PRICE
$2,530,000 (£1,345,745)

Opposite. *Jan Jansz. den Uyl,* Still Life on a Table with a White Cloth, *1633, oil on panel, 90 by 72 cm, sold 14 January 1988.*

PRICE
$2,200,000 (£1,170,213)

These seventeenth-century Dutch paintings, from the collection of Linda and Gerald Guterman, illustrate two different schools of still-life painting. Jan Davidsz. de Heem's elaborate still life exemplifies his interest in pictorial effects with a profusion of luscious foodstuffs and intricately crafted precious objects depicted in brilliant detail. Dated 1649, it was painted thirteen years after de Heem settled in Antwerp. According to Sandrant, the seventeenth-century historian, de Heem moved to the bustling and successful commercial city of Antwerp because 'there one could find rare fruits of all kinds ... in finer condition and state of ripeness to draw from life'. In this and other paintings, de Heem formulated an influential new style combining traditional elements of both Dutch and Flemish art. Jan Jansz. den Uyl's still life exhibits qualities of the other great tradition, the monochrome banquet-piece. In this masterwork of chromatic subtlety, restrained tonality and spare composition predominate. Here all the main elements are placed on the left side of the picture, balanced only by the strong architectural elements on the right.

THE ANDY WARHOL COLLECTION

'I really believe in empty spaces,' Andy Warhol maintained. 'I want to live in a studio. In one room. That's what I've always wanted, not to have anything – maybe put everything on microfilm or holographic wafers – and just move into one room.' But somehow the microfilming never took place and the shopping expeditions never stopped, and last April, Warhol's vast collections filled Sotheby's galleries in New York, a space totalling over three acres. One gallery displayed the American Indian art; four cases were required for the cookie jars; tables stacked with Fiesta ware lined the walls. An entire floor was devoted to the Art Deco collection, the American federal furniture, the folk art and the modern and contemporary paintings and drawings. Tucked away at one side were a dozen cases of watches and jewellery and parked outside on the corner was the Warhol Rolls Royce.

Much of the collection had been housed in a formal Georgian townhouse on East 66th Street in Manhattan, which Warhol claimed had once belonged to 'someone's Wasp granny'. This elegant setting, with its elaborately carved marble fireplaces, intricately stencilled walls, and luxurious damask draperies, was just as astonishing as the extent and variety of the collections within. The revelation of an unknown aspect of the life of such a prominent personality immediately captured the public imagination. In spite of his international celebrity, Warhol had remained elusive, essentially unengaged and aloof, and these objects and the secrets they might reveal about their owner were an intensely tantalizing prospect.

The basic sequence of Warhol's collecting is well known – Surrealist works

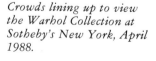

Crowds lining up to view the Warhol Collection at Sotheby's New York, April 1988.

Mary Shivers of Sotheby's Tribal Art Department setting up the exhibition of American Indian art from the Warhol Collection.

and American folk art in the fifties and early sixties, jewellery and watches in the mid-sixties and seventies, Art Deco in the early seventies, American Federal furniture in the mid-seventies to furnish the 66th Street house, and a late enthusiasm for sculpture of all periods from antiquity to the twentieth century. As an artist, he was naturally interested in the work of his contemporaries, acquiring important works by Twombly, Johns and Rauschenberg and his fellow Pop artists Lichtenstein and Rosenquist, and supported younger artists, Basquiat, Arman, and Haring among them. In *Popism*, Warhol recorded his encounters with Johns and Rauschenberg and some of his uncertainties and aspirations in dealing with his fellow artists. Henry Geldzahler, a former curator of twentieth-century art at the Metropolitan Museum of Art in New York, described the acquisition of such works as 'a deliberate gesture [that was] both a homage and a kind of

Right. *Exhibition of the Warhol Collection.*

Right. *Exhibition of American paintings and furniture from the Warhol Collection.*

apprenticeship to his fellow painters.' Perhaps the work which addresses his interaction with other artists most directly was the sensitive portrait drawn by David Hockney in Paris in 1974, the same year Warhol made a portrait of Hockney based on photographs taken during the visit.

In his collecting, Warhol has been variously described as an 'indefatigable accumulator', an 'obsessive hoarder', a 'manic bargain hunter' and a collector in the tradition of Lorenzo de Medici and William Randolph Hearst, 'knowingly following a pattern of profligate over-accumulation to be succeeded in good time by soul-searching de-acquisition.' He was a notorious shopper, usually spending two or three hours a day visiting galleries and auction houses and on Sundays the flea markets on the West Side. As Fred Hughes, his confidant and manager, once explained, Warhol believed shopping was part of his job. The search and the moment of acquisition were

Opposite. *Cookie jar exhibition.*

as important, if not more so, than the subsequent ownership of the object. In his friend Jed Johnson's view, he was 'in it for the action', and he especially loved the unpredictable nature of bidding in the saleroom.

Beneath the apparent randomness, Warhol's collecting pattern was surprisingly well defined. 'Andy was an omnivorous observer and recorder of everything and his collecting habits were in some ways an extension of this,' commented Fred Hughes. Just as he believed that ordinary people were entitled to a few moments of glory, so were commonplace objects worthy of serious if fleeting attention. 'The pursuit of masterpieces did not prevent him from finding objects of interest at all ranges of quality,' his shopping cohort Stuart Pivar observed. 'In the quest for bronzes of fine patination or ciselure, he would buy Rodin's *Le Penseur* in black glazed ceramic for $26 at the flea market.'

Perhaps the most remarkable aspect of Warhol as a collector was this versatility, the ability to turn with ease from one subject to another and to see the style – and very often the humour – in such extraordinarily diverse objects. Usually, in fact, he was among those who recognized it first, buying forties jewellery, Fiesta ware and American federal furniture before others 'rediscovered' them. Warhol's Art Deco collection was certainly the best example. Acquired in the early 1970s, largely in Paris as the market began to develop, this group included important pieces by Ruhlmann and Dunand as well as an exceptionally rare suite by Pierre Legrain. The wealth of handsomely designed silver by Puiforcat was discovered in a dusty showcase in their Paris showroom in 1969 and purchased en masse.

The Art Deco collection was the first to be auctioned, and throughout the ten-day sale, the bidders were just as diverse and unexpected as the objects they sought. A few, such as Gedalio Grinburg, now the world's cookie jar czar, and Matt Belgrano, a punk rocker with a scarlet mohawk who flew in from London for the event, became famous for just over the requisite fifteen minutes. Others were more circumspect, like the anonymous collector who paid $170,000, more than twenty times the estimate, for a tremendously stylish Egyptian revival chair.

Equally, the major pieces in the collection attracted serious international

Bidders at the Warhol sale.

competition. A European dealer purchased the Legrain consoles for a total of $418,000; the severe black centre table designed by Charles Rennie Mackintosh for Hill House brought a record $275,000 from an American private collector; a major East Coast museum acquired the elegant federal sideboard attributed to Joseph Barry of Philadelphia for $104,000. Among the jewellery and watches, the dramatic, overscaled designs of the forties were in great demand, with many pieces selling for four or five and in some cases ten times their estimates. Predictably, the highest prices were reserved for the contemporary art with an untitled work by Twombly reaching a record $990,000 and Johns's *Screen Piece* realizing $660,000. In all, the Warhol Collection totalled just over $25 million and the proceeds were donated to the Andy Warhol Foundation for the Visual Arts.

The Federal drawing room.

THE TORCELLO MOSAIC

A Byzantine mosaic of an Apostle's head from Santa Maria Assunta, Torcello, second half of the 11th century, height 47 cm, sold 9 July 1987.

PRICE
£264,000 ($421,740)

The Apostle's head, resplendent in gold and coloured tesserae, is one of the rarest pieces of mosaic ever to come onto the market, and an intriguing story of discovery is attached to it.

The mosaic was found recently by a parish priest, Father Reynolds, in the small church of St Anne, at Talygarn, mid-Glamorgan. Approaching the National Museum of Wales, Father Reynolds was referred to the Courtauld Institute's Byzantine expert Dr Robin Cormack, whose researches soon revealed that the head had come from the far right-hand corner of a row of apostles in the Last Judgement scene on the west wall of Santa Maria Assunta, formerly the Cathedral of Torcello. These are among the earliest mosaics in the Venice area, even pre-dating those of San Marco: the Apostle's head is dated *c.* 1070.

Torcello has shared with San Marco various episodes of restoration, particularly in the second half of the nineteenth century, and between 1852 and 1856, when the official restorer of the monuments, Giovanni Moro, was working at Torcello, certain sections of the original mosaics on the west wall were detached and replaced with pastiches. Whether or not Moro had licence to remove them remains unclear, since some portions were then considered too damaged to restore.

It was almost thirty years later that George Thomas Clarke, who built the church in Talygarn in memory of his wife, visited Italy, and more particularly Torcello. Clarke was a renowned engineer and archaeologist who had worked under Brunel on the building of the Great Western Railway. It was certainly prior to the building of the church in 1887–8, and probably on this trip to Italy, that he obtained the Apostle's head. He had it set securely within the brick masonry of the church, in the south transept, close to the family pew.

The successful sale was duly celebrated at Sotheby's: invitations to lunch were extended to the parish congregation, many of whom made the journey to London for the occasion.

THE SECRET TREATY OF DOVER

The secret Treaty of Dover was probably the most scandalous treaty ever negotiated by an English monarch. In return for substantial sums of money from Louis XIV, Charles II consented to become a Roman Catholic and to work towards the reconversion of the English nation. He agreed to use a French army if necessary to secure his position, to join with Louis in an offensive war against the Dutch, and to support Louis's claims to Spanish monarchical possessions in return for a division of the Spanish Empire.

It is possible that the treaty, had it been implemented, would have meant the end of rule by Parliament and of the Church of England. The English might also have come to govern not only North America but the greater part of Latin America as well.

In the event, Charles received large payments from Louis, which he used to build up the English navy, and avoided ever having to declare himself a Catholic. He was forced, however, into a futile and bloody war with the Dutch, thereby directly assisting French imperialist policies, without making any territorial acquisitions for himself.

Participation in the negotiations for this treaty was the most important step in the career of Thomas, 1st Lord Clifford of Chudleigh. Lord High Treasurer of England and acting Secretary of State in 1672–3, he was one of those ministers of Charles II known (from their combined initials) as the 'CABAL'. A Roman Catholic, he was commonly held to be the chief cause of the war with Holland, and it may be that a sense of guilt over this prompted his alleged suicide by hanging.

Secrecy surrounding the treaty was so closely maintained that the documents were never deposited in official archives, but entrusted instead to Clifford himself, then Charles's favourite minister. They remained in the family until the sale last year by the 13th Lord Clifford. Altogether, the Clifford Archive is among the most important collections of Restoration state papers to have remained in private hands.

A manuscript page from the secret Treaty of Dover, 1670, a collection of working drafts, memoranda, correspondence and agreements secretly preserved in the archive of Thomas, 1st Lord Clifford of Chudleigh (1630-73), Lord High Treasurer of England, concerning the negotiations for the Treaty, including signed protocols for the final ratified version, approximately 320 pages in all, sold 24 July 1987.

PRICE
£313,500 ($532,950)

IMPRESSIONIST AND MODERN PAINTINGS 1987–88

An auction of Impressionist and Modern Paintings in London on 30 June 1987. The lot being sold is André Derain's The Thames Embankment, *1906.*

PRICE
£990,000 ($1,593,900)

The impressionist market is international and dollar-based, with collectors in the US, Europe and Japan, and auctions centred in London and New York. Sotheby's evening sales of major Impressionist paintings – admission by ticket only, black tie, packed with celebrities and important collectors – are among the most exclusive occasions in the international art world, taking place at the height of the social seasons. The Impressionist sales from spring 1987 to spring 1988 took place against the background of a 'bull' market, with money made on the stock exchange channelled into intense competition for art. The brutal reversals caused by the stockmarket crash in October last year have made collectors more wary of mediocre work, even by distinguished painters, but have not depressed prices for top quality items. This is reflected in the record price of $53,900,000 paid for Van Gogh's 1889 painting *Irises* less than two weeks after the stock market crash. Japanese buying was strong throughout, with over twenty per cent of the sale total in London on 31 March accounted for by Japanese collectors.

Spring 1987 in New York saw the sale of Impressionist and Modern paintings from the collection of the late Sam Spiegel, the famous producer of such films as *On the Waterfront* and *Lawrence of Arabia*. Spiegel bought at the height of his career in the 1950s and early 1960s, when Impressionist paintings of the highest quality were more plentiful on the market. The fourteen lots included works by Picasso, Braque, Gris, Soutine and Chagall. A quarry by Cézanne, *Carrière de Bibémus*, c. 1898–1900, made $3,290,000. The current international enthusiasm for twentieth-century British painting was reflected in the $962,500 paid for Francis Bacon's *Pope No. 3*, 1960, double its estimate.

The Spiegel Collection was immediately followed by the major New York spring auction of Impressionist and Modern paintings. In a single evening $63,596,500 worth of art passed under the hammer, and amongst this, thirteen lots sold for over a million dollars each. This diverse sale had one very unusual feature: a rare portrait by the Vienna Secession painter Gustav Klimt, which went to a Japanese buyer for $3,850,000. The subject was Eugenia Primavesi, the wife of the banker Otto Primavesi, a major patron of the Wiener Werkstätte. The 1912 portrait is a superb example of Klimt's mature style, with a naturalistically treated head surrounded by the abstract patterns of the robe and background.

By coincidence, two Klimts from other sources were offered in the London sales of March and June, making equally spectacular prices. *Rose von Rosthorn-Friedmann*, painted eleven years earlier than *Eugenia Primavesi*, conveys with striking economy the Viennese *grande dame*, queen of the night in her cascade of sequins, boa and ropes of pearls (£1,760,000). The June sale contained the first Klimt landscape ever to appear at auction, *Schloss Kammer am Attersee II*, 1909. It made £3,300,000, a world record for the artist. The landscape shows the fashionable Austrian lakeside resort

Paul Cézanne, Carrière de Bibémus, *c. 1898–1900, oil on canvas, from the collection of the late Sam Spiegel, sold in New York 11 May 1987.*

PRICE
$3,290,000 (£1,981,928)

145

where Klimt spent many summers from 1897, the painting's teasing play between form and pattern presaging the stylization of *Eugenia Primavesi*. The season's remarkable group of Viennese paintings was complemented by Egon Schiele's 1909 portrait of his artist brother-in-law Anton Peschka (£1,760,000). Schiele's early, silvery study owes much to Klimt in its hypnotic

Gustav Klimt, Bildnis Eugenia (Mäda) Primavesi, *1912, oil on canvas, 140 by 85 cm, sold in New York 11 May 1987.*

PRICE
$3,850,000 (£2,319,277)

use of pattern, but the raw and tense hands betray his own more disturbing vision.

The term 'Impressionist and Modern Art' covers the key schools of the late nineteenth century and the first half of the twentieth century. Collectors in this field frequently assemble groups of paintings with considerable stylistic diversity, the criterion being that they are major works of art. In the 1987–8 season, mainstream Impressionism was represented by some superb paintings, such as Monet's *Le Jardin Fleuri*, 1900, a depiction of the artist's garden at Giverny painted with all the glowing colour of his late style. It sold in New York on 11 November to an American private buyer for $5,830,000, a world record for a Monet. The picture had been in the United States since 1915, when it was acquired from Monet's dealer, the Galerie Durand-Ruel in Paris, by Martin A. Ryerson of Chicago. American taste for Impressionism is of long standing, though today the market has broadened considerably.

Claude Monet, Le Jardin Fleuri, *signed and dated 1900, oil on canvas, 89 by 92 cm, sold in New York 11 November 1987.*

PRICE
$5,830,000 (£3,512,048)

147

Opposite. *Pablo Picasso,* Souvenir du Havre, *1912, signed on the reverse, oil on canvas, 80.7 by 53.8 cm, sold in London 1 December 1987.*

PRICE
£4,180,000 ($7,607,600)

The centrepiece of the 11 November sale was Van Gogh's *Irises*, which went to an undisclosed private collector for $53,900,000, setting a world auction record for a work of art this is unlikely to be broken quickly (see page 112). There were fears that October's stock market crash might affect the price, but it was proved that if an item is sufficiently rare and desirable it will attract intense competition. The mystique which Van Gogh holds for collectors is obvious but indefinable; a few months earlier, the Yasuda Fire and Marine Insurance Company of Japan had paid £26,750,000 for his *Sunflowers*.

Degas's bronze *Petite Danseuse de Quatorze Ans* sold in New York on 10 May 1988 for $10,120,000 (see page 118). The wax original, dressed in a real tutu, caused a furore on account of its insolent realism when exhibited by Degas at the sixth Impressionist exhibition in 1881. *La Petite Danseuse de Quatorze Ans* was the only one of Degas's sculptures exhibited in his lifetime; none was cast until after his death. This bronze is one of a limited number of casts made by the Hébrard Foundry in the 1920s. The excellence and rarity of these casts, and the provenance of the piece, which belonged to an important New York collector, Belle Linsky, ensured the exceptional price.

It was also a brilliant season for Picasso, with excellent examples from several key periods in his career. In the May 1987 New York sale a dazzling early flower painting, executed in 1910, doubled its estimate at $2,145,000. In the same sale was *La Maternité*, among the most moving of the monumental mother and child studies of the 1920s ($3,520,000). The sale in London on 1 December included a major Cubist work, *Souvenir du Havre*, which made £4,180,000. The painting combines objects encountered by Picasso on a trip to the Normandy seaport with Braque in the spring of 1912. The witty assemblage of Cubist 'souvenirs' influenced a wide circle of Picasso's followers and echoes of his ideas can be seen in Juan Gris's evocation of a bullfighter, *Le Torero*, 1913, which was sold in New York on 11 November for $1,980,000. As happens so often, a distinguished provenance influenced the price; the picture once belonged to Ernest Hemingway and was used as the frontispiece for his novel *Death in the Afternoon*. In May 1988 *Buste de Femme Souriante*, also from the Linsky Collection, brought $4,400,000.

The season included two unusual single artist sales: paintings by the architect Le Corbusier (see page 24) and the contents of the studio of René Magritte (see page 33). Other highlights included a vibrant still life by Matisse, *Nature Morte, Serviette à Carreaux*, c. 1903–4, one of his earliest fauve paintings, which incorporates a self-portrait of the painter reflected in a mirror (£1,250,000). The June sale in London contained one of Ben Nicholson's coolly enticing abstracts from the collection of the great connoisseur and art critic Lord Clark. Acquired by a German collector for £242,000, double its estimate, it showed another twentieth-century British painter rightfully recognized as a master of the modern school.

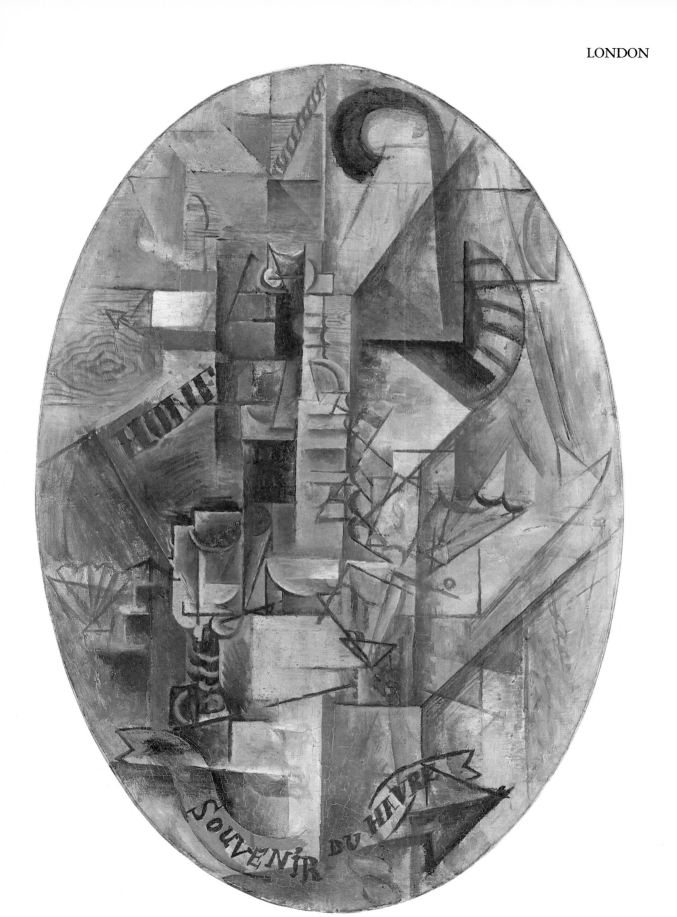

CLARE BOOTHE LUCE: 'LA LUCE AMERICANA'

Above. *Clare Boothe Luce wearing the Van Cleef & Arpels sapphire and diamond suite, which sold for a total of $145,750 (£77,000).*

Right. *Diamond Maltese cross brooch, Verdura, sold 19 April 1988.*

PRICE
$52,250 (£27,650)

An editor, playwright, Congresswoman, war correspondent and ambassador, Clare Boothe Luce was one of the most versatile and accomplished women of her generation. Her personal collection of jewels, objects of vertu, paintings and decorative works of art, which was dispersed in New York in the spring, reflected the variety of her life and her myriad personal and professional interests. Her jewels, for example, included elegant gold chains and simple earrings for the office, as well as a spectacular sapphire and diamond suite and an emerald and diamond necklace that would dazzle the most sophisticated diplomatic gathering. Perhaps the most evocative were the charms on her necklaces – Romulus and Remus for her time in Rome, a Southern Belle for the Luce plantation in South Carolina, the Capitol dome for her years in Congress, and many more.

Clare Boothe Luce's career as an editor and writer began at *Vogue*. After an initial rejection by Condé Nast, she simply arrived at the *Vogue* offices and created her own job on the magazine. Her talent as a writer was quickly recognized and she was transferred to *Vanity Fair*, where she became managing editor in 1933 at the age of 30. The years at *Vogue* and *Vanity Fair* had an important influence, introducing her to cultural and social leaders and heightening her own sense of style and fashion. Among her favourite jewels were two Maltese crosses by Verdura. He had originally introduced this motif for Coco Chanel and subsequently incorporated it on one of Diana Vreeland's signature bangles. With that endorsement, the Maltese cross became one of the most fashionable designs of 1940s jewellery.

In the early 1930s Clare met both Bernard Baruch, the powerful government adviser on economics, who became her great friend and mentor, and Henry R. Luce, then editor-in-chief of *Time* magazine and ultimately

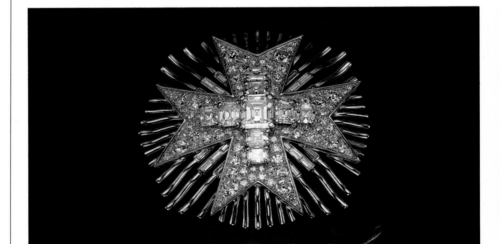

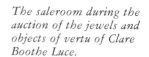

chairman of the Time-Life publishing empire. Luce, well known for his decisiveness, proposed to Clare after only a few meetings and they were married in 1935. Many of the pieces in her collection were gifts from her husband and several are inscribed for the occasion – a Cartier enamelled cross in 1948, given soon after her conversion to Catholicism, and a gold box presented for Valentine's Day in 1967.

Mrs Luce's literary career flourished throughout the 1930s. She published her first collection of short stories, and in 1939 she wrote three plays, *The Women*, *Kiss the Boys Goodbye* and *Margin for Error*. *The Women* enjoyed particular success and was produced around the world, including in Germany and Tokyo, and was recently revived on Broadway.

By the late 1930s, however, the threat of war commanded the attention of both Henry and Clare Luce. Following an investigative journey through Europe, Mrs Luce wrote her prophetic book *Europe in the Spring*, which reveals her perceptive insights into the situation and her awareness of the extreme threat of Nazism. After the outbreak of war, she accepted the position of war correspondent for *Life* magazine and travelled again through Europe and to the Far East. On her return, she ran for Congress and in 1942 was elected to the first of two consecutive terms in the House of Representatives. In 1953 she was offered the most important position of her career. President Eisenhower appointed her ambassador to Italy, the first woman to be an American envoy to a major country. She was so successful in the post that she was affectionately dubbed by the Italians 'La Luce Americana', the American Light.

When Henry Luce retired as publisher of Time-Life, Inc. in 1964, he and Clare moved to Phoenix, where they began to plan a magnificent estate in Hawaii. Mr Luce died before the house was completed, but his wife took up residence. She returned regularly to New York and Washington and remained politically active by supporting the Republican party and its leaders. In 1979 she was the first woman to receive West Point's Sylvanus Thayer Award, usually reserved for Generals and Secretaries of Defense.

The final and most prestigious tribute was bestowed on her by President Reagan in 1983 when he awarded her the Medal of Freedom, the highest civilian honour of the United States. Clare Boothe Luce died in October 1987 but her legacy to American women will be perpetuated through the Clare Boothe Luce Fund established to support women seeking careers in the sciences. The sale realized a total of $2,164,000.

GREAT LITTLE SALES

The headline-grabbing million pound or dollar record has become almost a daily occurrence in the saleroom, but the stories attached to many less expensive lots are often just as interesting. The experts in the departments derive considerable satisfaction on behalf of a client if they can achieve a high price, but if the client happens to be a pensioner and the lot makes £2,000 instead of the expected £1,000, the satisfaction is of a different order. These stories are only occasionally reported, and more often locally than nationally.

While hundreds of people daily take advantage of Sotheby's free service of advice at the salerooms and offices, experts are also regularly sent out throughout Europe on specialized 'Discovery Days'. These are advertized in the Press and take place in local halls or hotels. Unless run in conjunction with a registered charity, in which case an entrance charge is made, they are also free. These events provide a wealth of material, and stories to accompany them. Neil Davey, Director of the Japanese department, visited a client in Vienna after one such day and unearthed an unrecognized ivory *netsuke* by Gechu, a rare late-eighteenth century carver. It subsequently made a world-record price of £100,000. At another event, in Torquay, David Bennett, Director of the Jewellery Department in London, searched patiently through a jewel-box full of minor pieces. The owner was most disappointed that there was nothing of great value, and only on being prompted revealed that there was a bracelet 'of small value' in the bottom of the case. She knew it was not worth showing to him, as a local jeweller had estimated it at a few hundred pounds.

Bennett recognized it as the work of Fasoli, a jeweller about whom little is known, who was active in Italy in the second half of the nineteenth century. At this period craftsmen in ceramics, furniture and silver as well as jewellers were much influenced by the neo-classical revival. The bracelet, in gold, with fine granulation and wirework is a typical, high-quality piece. The owner was not a little amazed to find her bracelet re-estimated at £3,000–4,000. It fetched £5,500.

A block of five Penny Black stamps, plate 8, 1840, sold 24 November 1987.

PRICE
£6,600 ($11,352)

The happy accident strikes with encouraging frequency in the art world and many chance discoveries come under the hammer every year. In November 1987 the stamp department handled the sale of the third largest block of 1840 Penny Blacks, from plate 8, one of the rarest plates on record. This block of five of the earliest postage stamps ever produced had survived in perfect condition preserved between the pages of a dictionary, to be rediscovered some one hundred and forty years later, when the owner decided to rebind the book. The block sold for £6,600.

A more puzzling find was of a mid-fifteenth century ceremonial arrowhead in the form of a cross-bow bolt. This was unearthed in South Africa and used for some while by the owners' gardener as a tool for weeding and trimming the edge of the lawn. There is no satisfactory explanation of how such a rare and early weapon came to be buried in the Cape. It sold for £9,350.

The sale of items of family history is often tinged with sadness, particularly when the piece is as personal as a medal awarded for outstanding gallantry, and most of all when the award is posthumous. In 1968 Barbara Jane Harrison, a stewardess, lost her life trying to save passengers from a burning aircraft at Heathrow. She was awarded the George Cross, one of only four ever awarded to women and the only one since the last war. Her father was forced to sell the medal to help support the rest of the family. It fetched £9,900 in October 1987.

Close personal association with the famous is a factor which frequently generates high prices, and it is difficult to get much closer than the clothes they wore. Sotheby's auctioned the costumes from Diaghilev's Ballets Russes in 1967, among them Nijinksy's costume for the Blue God, designed by Leon Bakst, which sold for £900. When it reappeared last October, it was perhaps the only costume not in a museum that had been worn by the great dancer. It was still as it was when Nijinsky removed it for the last time before the end of the First World War, his name on the lining, and blue make-up on the collar. It was bought by the Australian National Gallery for £6,600.

Interest in theatrical material and memorabilia of all sorts has increased enormously in the last few years including mementoes of such rock and roll heroes as the Beatles. In November 1968, two students at Loughborough University wrote to John Lennon asking if they could talk to him about his political philosophy. In December that year they taped, on their own cassette recorder, two hours of Lennon expounding his often witty and forthright views on just about every subject ranging from religion and politics to LSD and macrobiotic diets. There were revealing comments on the Beatles and the Apple Organisation, money and happiness. Yoko Ono was present for part of the interview and added some comments, but it was almost entirely two hours of unadulterated and, more importantly, unpublished Lennon.

In August 1987 the students, now middle-aged, decided to sell. The tapes were electronically enhanced and sold with signed affidavits granting all copyright to the purchaser. Such is the strength of Beatlemania and particularly the almost mystical awe in which Lennon is held that, against an estimate of £7,000–9,000, they sold for £23,650 to an American buyer.

This is no place to raise the thorny problem of returning works of art to their country of origin. Suffice it to say that they have been used as international exchange for thousands of years and museums would be exceptionally dull were they unable to display and contrast the finest examples of all cultures. An extraordinary illustration of the way in which works of art make their way to and from the most unlikely places was

Tibetan Thang-ka, *19th century, paint on cloth, 1.22 m by 83.5 cm, sold 23 November 1987.*

PRICE
£7,100 ($13,490)

demonstrated last year. A Swedish client brought in a collection of Chinese porcelain and a Tibetan *Thang-ka* (pronounced 'tanker').

The Swedes were among explorers from many nations who visited Africa, India and the Chinese sub-continent in the second half of the last century. They made their way to Tibet overland via Russia and brought back many souvenirs of their travels. In this case the owner was unaware of what the piece was, or that it had much value.

While *Thang-kas* are not uncommon, this example was unusual on several counts. It was exceptionally large, very finely painted and the iconography was particularly interesting. *Than-kas* are religious paintings hung on the walls of monasteries or temples as an aid to contemplation and usually depict one of the ferocious Buddhistic gods, typical of the Tibetan form of the religion, who protected the monks and monastery. The centre is an offering below five deities flying in a sky amongst human heads trailing tatters of skin. Wood is so precious a commodity on the high Tibetan plateau that it cannot be used for cremation and the bodies of the dead are exposed on the bare rock to be picked over by the vultures depicted below them. At the foot of the painting are skulls, severed heads and limbs adrift in a sea of blood. Despite its extremely gruesome subject, the *Thang-ka* made £7,100 against an estimate of £1,500–2,000.

In Autumn 1986 two grubby bottles were left with our wine department. They bore considerable wear, the labels were scratched and dirty with an inscription in a wobbly hand which declared: 'Port, Biggs Dorchester, 1868'.

Ports of this age would be worth about £80–£120 per bottle. David Molyneux-Berry MW, the director of the department, was not entirely convinced of their authenticity on several grounds: the paper appeared too recent, the wear on the bottles suggested they had been in a stream or the sea, and close examination revealed that the considerable acccumulation of dirt had been sprayed on. Furthermore the seal seemed to be dyed candlewax rather than the hard black material to be expected. They were consigned to the tasting-room to await further inspection. The following Monday there was a loud explosion from the tasting-room and a quick bomb check revealed nothing more than one of the bottles spewing pink foam over the carpet. No Master of Wine can resist an open bottle and the unprogrammed tasting revealed not vintage port but a very recent Lambrusco, a semi-sparkling Italian red wine. The owner was contacted and no more was heard.

Some weeks later while checking the wines at Sotheby's Billingshurst, Molyneux-Berry was horrified to spot two similar wax seals lying in the bins. This time the label was a much more professional, printed job and the contents were stated to be Croft 1924. The bottles contained cheap port diluted with home-brewed wine. They had been consigned by the same owner. Now very worried, Molyneux-Berry informed Sotheby's security on return to Bond Street, who in turn contacted the local police. They drew a blank.

Sometime later there was a telephone call from Billingshurst – the man was back with two further bottles of the same wine. On instructions from Bond Street, they were booked in for sale as normal and the police again informed. They turned up at the man's house just as he returned from the local supermarket with another batch of cheap wines.

In court it was revealed that he had been practising the deception for some time and that other salerooms in London and elsewhere had unknowingly sold his unpleasant mixture. Moral: never judge a wine by its label – it is not necessarily what it purports to be.

Three forged bottles of port.

DURER'S MELENCOLIA

*M*elencolia, Durer's most complex engraving, has been characterized by art historian Erwin Panofsky as a psychological self-portrait. Durer had in fact become the first western artist to paint a self-portrait when at the age of thirteen, in 1484, he drew a portrait of himself from the mirror. This exceptionally rich impression, from the collection of the Kimbell Art Foundation in Fort Worth, Texas, brought a world record price.

Albrecht Durer, Melencolia *(B. 74; Holl 75), 1514, engraving, 24.1 by 18.9 cm, sold 13 May 1987.*

PRICE
$511,500 (£308,133)

PRINCIPAL OFFICERS, EXPERTS AND REPRESENTATIVES

The Rt. Hon. The Earl of Gowrie
Chairman, Sotheby's UK
John L. Marion
Chairman, Sotheby's North America
Julian Thompson
Chairman, Sotheby's International
Diana D. Brooks
President, Sotheby's North America
Timothy Llewellyn
Managing Director, Sotheby's UK
Simon de Pury
Managing Director, Sotheby's Europe

American Decorative Arts and Furniture
Leslie B. Keno *New York, 606 7130*
William W. Stahl, Jnr *606 7110*

American Folk Art
Nancy Druckman *New York, 606 7225*

American Indian Art
Dr Bernard de Grunne
New York, 606 7325

American Paintings, Drawings and Sculpture
Peter B. Rathbone *New York, 606 7280*

Antiquities and Asian Art
Richard M. Keresey
New York, 606 7328
Felicity Nicholson (Antiquities)
London, 408 5111
Brendan Lynch (Asian) *408 5112*

Arms and Armour
Michael Baldwin *London, 408 5318*
Florian Eitle *New York, 606 7250*

Books and Manuscripts
Roy Davids *London, 408 5287*
David N. Redden *New York, 606 7386*
Dominique Laucournet
Paris, 33 (1) 42 66 40 60

British Paintings 1500–1850
James Miller *London, 408 5405*
Henry Wemyss (Watercolours)
408 5409

British Paintings from 1850
Simon Taylor (Victorian)
London, 408 5385
Janet Green (20th Century) *408 5387*

Ceramics
Peter Arney *London, 408 5134*
Letitia Roberts *New York, 606 7180*

Chinese Art
Carol Conover *New York, 606 7332*
Mee Seen Loong
Arnold Chang (Paintings) *606 7334*
Julian Thompson *London, 408 5371*
Colin Mackay *408 5145*
Robert Kleiner (Hong Kong sales) *408 5149*

Clocks and Watches
Tina Millar (Watches) *London, 408 5328*
Michael Turner (Clocks) *408 5329*
Daryn Schnipper *New York, 606 7162*

Coins and Medals
Tom Eden (Ancient and Islamic)
London, 408 5313
James Morton (English and Paper Money) *408 5314*
David Erskine-Hill (Medals and Decorations) *408 5315*
Mish Tworkowski *New York, 606 7391*

Collectables
Dana Hawkes *New York, 606 7424*
Hilary Kay *London, 408 5205*

Contemporary Art
Hugues Joffre *London, 408 5400*
Lucy Mitchell-Innes *New York, 606 7254*

European Works of Art
Elizabeth Wilson *London, 408 5321*
Florian Eitle *New York, 606 7250*

Furniture
Graham Child *London, 408 5347*
George Read (English) *New York, 606 7577*
Thierry Millerand (French and Continental) *606 7213*
Robert C. Woolley *606 7100*
Alexandre Pradère
Paris, 33 (1) 42 66 40 60

Glass and Paperweights
Lauren Tarshis *New York, 606 7180*
Perran Wood *London, 408 5135*

Impressionist and Modern Paintings
David J. Nash *New York, 606 7351*
John L. Tancock *606 7360*
Marc E. Rosen (Drawings) *606 7154*
Michel Strauss *London, 408 5389*
Julian Barran
Paris, 33 (1) 42 66 40 60

Islamic Art and Carpets
Richard M. Keresey (Works of Art) *New York, 606 7328*
William F. Ruprecht (Carpets), *606 7380*
John Carswell *London, 408 5153*

Japanese Art
Peter Bufton *New York, 606 7338*
Neil Davey *London, 408 5141*

Jewellery
David Bennett *London, 408 5306*
John D. Block *New York, 606 7392*
Nicholas Rayner *Geneva, 41 (22) 32 85 85*

Judaica
Jay Weinstein *New York, 606 7387*

Latin American Paintings
Anne Horton *New York, 606 7290*

Musical Instruments
Charles Rudig *New York, 606 7190*
Graham Wells *London, 408 5341*

19th Century European Furniture and Works of Art
Christopher Payne
London, 408 5350
Elaine Whitmire
New York, 606 7285

19th Century European Paintings and Drawings
Alexander Apsis *London, 408 5384*
Nancy Harrison *New York, 606 7140*
Pascale Pavageau *Paris, 33 (1) 42 66 40 60*

Old Master Paintings and Drawings
Timothy Llewellyn
London, 408 5373
Julien Stock *408 5420*
Elizabeth Llewellyn (Drawings) *408 5416*
George Wachter *New York, 606 7230*
Alexander Nystadt
Amsterdam, 31 (20) 27 56 56
Nancy Ward-Neilson *Milan, 39 (2) 783911*
Etienne Breton *Paris, 33 (1) 42 66 40 60*

Oriental Manuscripts
Nabil Saidi *London, 408 5332*

Photographs
Philippe Garner *London, 408 5138*
Beth Gates-Warren *New York, 606 7240*

Portrait Miniatures, Objects of Vertu, Icons and Russian Works of Art
Martyn Saunders-Rawlins (Icons)
London, 408 5325
Julia Clarke (Vertu) *408 5324*
Haydn Williams (Miniatures) *408 5326*
Heinrich Graf von Spreti
Munich, 49 (89) 22 23 75
Gerard Hill *New York, 606 7150*

Postage Stamps
John Michael *London, 408 5223*

Pre-Columbian Art
Stacy Goodman *New York, 606 7330*

Prints
Marc E. Rosen *New York, 606 7117*
Ian Mackenzie *London, 408 5210*

Silver
Kevin L. Tierney *New York, 606 7160*
Peter Waldron (English) *London, 408 5104*
Harold Charteris (Continental) *408 5106*
Christoph Graf Douglas
Frankfurt, 49 (69) 740787

Sporting Guns
James Booth *London, 408 5319*

Tribal Art
Dr Bernard de Grunne

New York, 606 7325
Roberto Fainello *London, 408 5115*

20th Century Applied Arts
Barbara E. Deisroth *New York, 606 7170*
Philippe Garner
London, 408 5138

Vintage Cars
Malcolm Barber *London, 408 5320*
Dana Hawkes *New York, 606 7424*

Western Manuscripts
Dr Christopher de Hamel, FSA
London, 408 5330

Wine
David Molyneux Berry, MW
London, 408 5267
Christopher Ross *408 5271*

UK AND IRELAND

London
34–35 New Bond Street,
London W1A 2AA
Telephone: (01) 493 8080
and Bloomfield Place
(off New Bond Street)
Telephone: (01) 493 8080
Telex: 24454 SPBLON G

Chester
Richard Allen
Booth Mansion,
28 Watergate Street,
Chester, Cheshire CH1 2NA
Telephone: (0244) 315531
Telex: 61577 SOBART G

Sussex
W. L. Weller, FRICS, FSLVA
Summers Place, Billingshurst,
Sussex RH14 9AD
Telephone: (040381) 3933
Telex: 87210 GAVEL

South and South West of England, Midlands and South Wales
John Harvey
18 Imperial Square, Cheltenham,
Gloucestershire GL50 1QZ
Telephone: (0242) 510500
George Kidner
42 Holdenhurst Road,
Bournemouth, Dorset BH8 8AF
Telephone: (0202) 294425
Mary Fagan
Basingstoke, Hampshire
Telephone: (0256) 780639
The Hon. Lady Butler
Warwick *Telephone: (0926) 651950*

Devon and Cornwall
John Tremlett
Bickham House
Kenn, Exeter EX6 7XL
Telephone: (0392) 833416

East of England
Christopher Myers
56 High Street, Trumpington,
Cambridge CB2 1LS
Telephone: (0223) 845222
Lady Victoria Leatham
George Archdale

157

George Hotel Mews, Station Road,
Stamford, Lincolnshire PE9 2LB
Telephone: (0780) 51666
The Lord Cranworth
Woodbridge, Suffolk
Telephone: (047 335) 581

North of England
John Phillips
Henrietta Graham
8–12 Montpellier Parade,
Harrogate, North Yorkshire HG1
2TJ
Telephone: (0423) 501466/7
Susan Yorke
Hall Foot, Worston, Clitheroe,
Lancashire BB7 1QA
Telephone: (0200) 41520
The Earl of Carlisle, MC, FRICS
Market Place, Brampton,
Cumbria CA8 1NW
Telephone: (069 77) 3666
Matthew Festing
11 Osborne Terrace, Jesmond,
Newcastle upon Tyne NE1 1NE
Telephone: (091) 2818867

Scotland
John Robertson
112 George Street,
Edinburgh EH2 4LH
Telephone: (031) 226 7201
Anthony Weld Forester
146 West Regent Street,
Glasgow G2 2RQ
Telephone: (041) 221 4817
Marquess of Huntly
Aberdeenshire
*Telephone: Banchory (033 02)
4007*

Ireland
William Montgomery
The Estate Office, Greyabbey,
Newtownards, Co. Down
Telephone: (024 774) 668
William Montgomery
123a Upper Abbey Street, Dublin 1
Telephone: (01) 734811
Julia Keane
Cappoquin, Co. Waterford
Telephone: (058) 54258

Channel Islands
Daan Cevat, MBE
3 Clos Des Fontaines,
La Villette, St Martin's, Guernsey,
CI
Telephone: (0481) 38009

UNITED STATES

New York
1334 York Avenue,
New York, NY 10021
Telephone: (212) 606 7000
Telex: 232643 (SPB UR)

Atlanta *(Associate)*
Virginia Groves Beach
Telephone: (404) 233 4928

Baltimore
Aurelia Bolton
Telephone: (301) 583 8864

Beverly Hills
Grace Lowe Russak
Barbara Pallenberg
Lisa Hubbard
Christine Eisenberg
Eleanore Phillips Colt
308 North Rodeo Drive,
Beverly Hills, California 90210
Telephone: (213) 274 0340

Boston
Patricia Ward
101 Newbury Street,
Boston, Massachusetts 02116
Telephone: (617) 247 2851

Chicago
Helyn Goldenberg
Gary Schuler
325 West Huron Street, Suite 205,
Chicago, Illinois 60610
Telephone: (312) 664 6800

Dallas
Mary Lide Kehoe
Telephone: (214) 361 6662

Hawaii
Andrea Song Gelber
Telephone: (808) 732 0122

Houston
Martha Farish
Telephone: (713) 528 2863

New Orleans
Debe Cuevas Lykes
Telephone: (504) 523 7059

Newport
Marion Oates Charles
Betsy D. Ray
Telephone: (401) 846 8668

New York City
Mrs Watson K. Blair
Virginia Guest
C. Hugh Hildesley
Lee Copley Thaw
Alastair A. Stair
Telephone: (212) 606 7110

Palm Beach
Hope P. Kent
Robert V. Ruggierio (Trusts &
Estates)
Susan Sencer
John Goldsmith Phillips
155 Worth Avenue,
Palm Beach, Florida 33480
Telephone: (305) 833 2582

Philadelphia
Wendy T. Foulke
Anne Sims
1811 Chestnut Street,
Philadelphia, Pennsylvania 19103
Telephone: (215) 751 9540

San Francisco
Mrs Prentis Cobb Hale
Mrs John N. Rosekrans
Teresa Hess-Nageotte
3667 Sacramento Street,
San Francisco, California 94118
Telephone: (415) 561 8409

Santa Fe
Julie Michel
Telephone: (505) 982 1637

Washington
Sara Dwyer
Marion Oates Charles
Penne Percy Korth
Joan F. Tobin
3201 New Mexico Ave NW, Suite
210, Washington, DC 20016
Telephone: (202) 363 5544

CANADA

Toronto
Christina Orobetz *(President)*
9 Hazelton Avenue,
Toronto, Ontario M5R 2EI
Telephone: (416) 926 1774

Montreal
Susan Travers
Telephone: (514) 934 1879

CENTRAL AMERICA

Mexico
Suzy De Gilly *(Public Relations
Associate)*
Calle Varsovia 226, Apt 301
Mexico 06600 DF
*Telephone: 52 (905) 511 3768 or
525 4263*
Françoise Reynaud *(Art
Consultant)*
Kepler 189, Mexico 11590 DF
Telephone: 52 (905) 5456971

LATIN AMERICA

Argentina
Mallory Hathaway de Gravière
Av. Quintana 475, Buenos Aires
Telephone: 54 (1) 804 9347
William R. Edbrooke
Kerteux Antiques,
Libertad 846, Buenos Aires
Telephone: 54 (1) 393 0831

Brazil
Walter Greyerhahn
Rua do Rosario 155–2° andar,
Rio de Janeiro 20041
Telephone: 55 (21) 222 7771
Heloise Guinlé, Rio de Janeiro
Telephone: 55 (21) 552 5769
Cornelius O. K. Reichenheim
Alameda Ministro Rocha
Azevedo 391, São Paulo 01410
*Telephone: 55 (11) 282 1599/
0581*
Pedro Correa do Lago
Rua João Cachoeira, 267,
04535 São Paulo SP
Telephone: 55 (11) 282 3135

FAR EAST

Hong Kong
Suzanne Tory
901–5 Lane Crawford House,
70 Queen's Road Central, Hong
Kong
Telephone: 852 (5) 248121

Taiwan, ROC
Rita Wong
49 An Ho Road, 4th Floor,
Taipei, Taiwan, ROC
Telephone: 886 (2) 776 1991

Japan
Kazuko Shiomi
Imperial Hotel, 1–1, Uchisaiwaicho
1–chome, Chiyoda-ku, Tokyo 100
Telephone: 81 (3) 504 1111

Singapore
Quek Chin Yeow
02–15, Hilton International
581 Orchard Road, Singapore 0923
Telephone: (65) 732 8239

EUROPE

Austria
Dr Agnes Husslein
Palais Breuner, Singerstrasse 16,
1010 Vienna
*Telephone: 43 (222) 524772/
524773*

Belgium
Count Henry de Limburg Stirum
32 Rue de l'Abbaye, Brussels 1050
Telephone: 32 (2) 343 50 07

Denmark
Baroness Hanne Wedell-
Wedellsborg
Bredgade 27, 1260 Copenhagen K,
Denmark
Telephone: 45 (1) 135556

France
Julian Barran
Alexandre Pradère
Anne de Lacretelle
Princesse Laure de Beauvau Craon
3 Rue de Miromesnil 75008, Paris
Telephone: 33 (1) 4 266 4060

Germany
Dr Christoph Graf Douglas
(Managing Director Germany)
*Telephone Frankfurt: 49 (69)
740787*
Johannes Ernst
Beethoven Strasse 71, D-6000,
Frankfurt-am-Main 1
Telephone: 49 (69) 740787
Ursula Niggemann
St Apern-Strasse 17–29
(Kreishaus Galerie), D-5000
Cologne 1
Telephone: 49 (221) 23 52 84/85
Ballindamm 17, 2000 Hamburg 1
Telephone: 49 (40) 33 75 53
Heinrich Graf von Spreti
Odeonsplatz 16, D-8000 Munich
22
Telephone: 49 (89) 2913151

Holland
Jan Pieter Glerum
Malcolm Barber
John Van Schaik
102 Rokin, 1012 KZ Amsterdam
Telephone: 31 (20) 27 5656

Hungary
Sotheby's Information Centre
Novotrade Inc., Kallman u. 16,
Budapest
Telephone: 36 (1) 113448

Italy
Michael Thomson-Glover
Palazzo Capponi
Via Gino Capponi
26, 50121 Florence
Telephone: 39 (55) 2479021
Bruno Muheim
Via Pietro Mascagni 15/2,
20121 Milan
Telephone: 39 (2) 783911
Giuseppe Ceccatelli
Piazza di Spagna 90, 00186 Rome
*Telephone: 39 (6) 678 1798 &
678 2734*
Laura Russo
Corso Galileo Ferraris 18B, 10100
Turin
Telephone: 39 (11) 544898

Monaco
Léon Leroy
BP 45, Le Sporting d'Hiver,
Place du Casino, MC 98001,
Monaco Cedex
Telephone: 33 (93) 30 88 80

Norway
Ingeborg Astrup
Bjornveien 42, 0387 Oslo 3,
Norway
Telephone: 47 (2) 1472 82

Portugal
Frederico Horta e Costa
Casa de S. Miguel,
Avenida da Franca, 2765 Estoril
Telephone: 351 (1) 267 0611

Spain
Edmund Peel
Plaza de la Independencia 8, 28001
Madrid
Telephone: 34 (1) 522 2902
Rocio Tassara
Luis Monreal Tejada *(Associate)*
Centro de Anticuarios no. 40,

Paseo de Gracia 55–57,
08007 Barcelona
Telephone: 34 (3) 215 2008/2149

Sweden and Finland
Hans Dyhlén
Arsenalsgatan 4, 111 47
Stockholm,
Sweden
Telephone: 46 (8) 101478/101479

Switzerland
Simon de Pury
(Chairman Switzerland)

*Telephone Geneva: 41 (22) 32 85
85*
Nicholas Rayner
13 Quai du Mont Blanc,
CH 1201 Geneva
Telephone: 41 (22) 32 85 85
Ully Wille
20 Bleicherweg, CH-8022 Zurich
Telephone: 41 (1) 202 0011

Israel
Rivka Saker
Daniella Luxembourg
38 Gordon St, Tel Aviv 63414,

Israel
*Telephone: 972 (3) 223822/
246897*

AUSTRALIA

Robert Bleakley
13 Gurner Street, Paddington,
Sydney, NSW 2021
Telephone: 61 (2) 332 3500
Ann Roberts, 606 High Street,
East Prahran, Melbourne, Victoria
3181
Telephone: 61 (3) 529 7999

ACKNOWLEDGEMENTS

We gratefully acknowledge the contributions of Tim Ayers, Susan Morris and Susan Rosenfeld of Sotheby's London and Christopher Apostle, Barbara Klein, Lynn Stowell Pearson and Martha Sullivan of Sotheby's New York in the compilation of this book.

PICTURE ACKNOWLEDGEMENTS

111 reproduced by William Connelly, *The True Chesterfield*, London 1939; 150 © Horst; 112, 114, 136, 137, 138 (2), 139 © Helaine Messer; 26 Musée de Versailles/© Roger Viollet; 56 Popperfoto; 78 courtesy Harry Winston, Inc.